BURY METRO LIBRARIES

This book must be returned on or before the last date recorded below to the Library from which it was borrowed.

AUTHOR

CLASS No.

TITLE

RADCLIFFE

RENEWALS

BOOK No.

0161 253 7160

Raw & Natural Nutrition *for* Dogs

The Definitive Guide to Homemade Meals

LEW OLSON

DharmaCafé Books

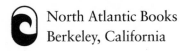

North Atlantic Books
Berkeley, California

Published by
North Atlantic Books   DharmaCafé
P.O. Box 12327   P.O. Box 1289
Berkeley, California 94712   Cobb, California 95426

Cover photo © iStockphoto.com/cynoclub
Cover and book design by Suzanne Albertson

Printed in the United States of America

Raw & Natural Nutrition for Dogs: The Definitive Guide to Homemade Meals is sponsored by the Society for the Study of Native Arts and Sciences, a nonprofit educational corporation whose goals are to develop an educational and cross-cultural perspective linking various scientific, social, and artistic fields; to nurture a holistic view of arts, sciences, humanities, and healing; and to publish and distribute literature on the relationship of mind, body, and nature.

DharmaCafé Books' publications are available through most bookstores. For further information, visit our website at www.dharmacafe.com.

North Atlantic Books' publications are available through most bookstores. For further information, visit our website at www.northatlanticbooks.com or call 800-733-3000.

Library of Congress Cataloging-in-Publication Data

Olson, Lew.
    Raw & natural nutrition for dogs : the definitive guide to homemade meals / Lew Olson.
        p. cm.
    Summary: "The first comprehensive book to cover both raw and home-cooked diets specifically for dogs, written by an expert in dog food research and development"—Provided by publisher.
    ISBN 978-1-55643-903-2
    1. Dogs—Food—Recipes. 2. Dogs—Nutrition. I. Title. II. Title: Raw and natural nutrition for dogs.
    SF427.4.O57 2010
    636.7'085—dc22
                                                    2010005078

5 6 7 8 9 10 11 Versa 16 15 14 13 12
Printed on recycled paper

For the Bean, Berte, Danny, and Iris

Contents

Introduction   ix

Part I: Nutrition Basics   1

Chapter One: The Untold History of Dog Food   3
Chapter Two: Canine and Digestion Anatomy
  Made Simple   13
Chapter Three: Protein Is a Dog's Best Friend   17
Chapter Four: The Real Low-Carb Revolution   23
Chapter Five: Fats for Canine Health   29
Chapter Six: Getting the Mineral Balance Right   34
Chapter Seven: Vitamins and Supplements for
  Canine Health   45

Part II: Feeding Your Dog the Easy Way   55

Chapter Eight: Feeding Homemade Diets the Easy Way   57
Chapter Nine: Feeding Raw the Easy Way   64
Chapter Ten: Feeding Cooked Diets the Easy Way   72
Chapter Eleven: No Quibble with Kibble   78
Chapter Twelve: Feeding Your Puppy   82
Chapter Thirteen: Feeding Senior Dogs   92
Chapter Fourteen: Diet and Pregnancy   95
Chapter Fifteen: Feeding on the Go   101
Chapter Sixteen: Working Dog Diets   105
Chapter Seventeen: Why Your Dog Is Not a Vegetarian   110
Chapter Eighteen: Picky Eaters   115

Part III: Remedial Diets Made Simple   121

A Guide to this Section   122
Chapter Nineteen: Heart-Healthy Diets   123
Chapter Twenty: Diets for Dogs with Cancer   132
Chapter Twenty-One: Diets for Kidney Needs   141

Chapter Twenty-Two: Diets for Liver Needs   150

Chapter Twenty-Three: Diet and Pancreatitis   158

Chapter Twenty-Four: Low-Glycemic Diets   165

Chapter Twenty-Five: Diet and Skin Problems   176

Chapter Twenty-Six: Diet and Joint Problems   180

Chapter Twenty-Seven: Diets for Bladder Health   187

Chapter Twenty-Eight: Diet and Gastric Problems   198

Chapter Twenty-Nine: Diet and the Immune System   207

Notes   213

Index   219

Acknowledgments   226

About the Author   227

Introduction

Christie Keith is contributing editor for Pet Connection *and writes the online pet care column for the* San Francisco Chronicle, *as well as the "Your Whole Pet" column twice monthly. She is the past director and editor of* America Online's Pet Care Forum, *editor of the* Veterinary Information Network's *pet owner website, and the founding editor of* VeterinaryPartner.com. *She has written numerous articles on pet health care and has bred, owned, and shown Scottish Deerhounds under the kennel name Caber Feidh.*

I'm a contributing editor for Universal Press Syndicate's *Pet Connection,* and helped cover the 2007 pet food recall for our nationally syndicated column and blog. Thousands of people came to our site during the many months of "rolling recalls," desperate for information on how to safely and nutritiously feed their dogs a homemade diet.

Most of these people had been convinced such a thing was all but impossible, that dogs have such mysterious and precise nutritional needs that only scientists are capable of formulating their diets, and only pet food manufacturers are capable of producing them.

But I knew different. I'd been feeding my own pets homemade diets for more than twenty-one years at that point. So I wasn't surprised when many of those people discovered that it was not as difficult as they'd been told, nor did it surprise me when they found that making that change triggered many improvements in their dogs' health.

Lew Olson is one of the first people I "met" years ago when the Internet and its thousands of email lists, message boards, and forums first made it possible for people all over the country and the world to communicate easily about how we were caring for our dogs. Lew and I struck up an online friendship that later became an offline one, largely because we shared a similar philosophy about homemade dog diets.

That philosophy, which is the foundation of this book, is that feeding a nutritious, wholesome homemade diet to our dogs is neither as difficult as we've been told, nor as foolproof as some "dog nutrition gurus" would suggest. That's because while it may be true that it's no more difficult to make your dog's food at home than it is to make your own, it's also no easier. Many people don't do a great job of making nutritional choices for themselves, mostly because modern life leaves them short on time and energy, and because we live in a culture of convenience. However, as Lew points out, when humans hit the fast food lane, we know we're doing it because it's easy and don't fool ourselves that it's because it's better for us. The opposite has become true with our pets; we've come to see packaged convenience foods as the nutritious choice for them, even while we know that a fresh, varied diet is the nutritious choice for us.

In this book you'll not only discover why dogs do best on a fresh, varied diet just like we do, but get easy detailed instructions on how to provide one. Lew gives specific recipes, supplement recommendations, and simple steps you can take to make sure you don't over- or under-supply your dog's nutritional needs.

But basic information isn't all you'll find in these pages. Lew outlines nutritional concepts that will enable you to evaluate canine nutritional information on your own, as well as to make sense of the often-conflicting advice provided by pet food manufacturers, veterinarians, dog breeders, pet store employees, people you meet at the dog park, and the Internet's thousands of "experts."

Like me, Lew believes there is no "one true way" to feed a dog, and thus her book is refreshingly free of dogma. Want to include raw meat and bones in your dog's diet? She tells you how. Want to feed raw meat, but without bones? She tells you how to do that, too. She also tells you how to feed balanced cooked diets. And then she does something a generation of pet food industry propaganda has been trying to convince us can't be done: tells us how to safely and nutritiously add fresh foods to your dog's kibble.

I've seen literally hundreds of dogs over the last two-plus decades whose health and quality of life have been revitalized by the switch to a homemade diet, or even just the addition of fresh foods to a commercial diet. Since the pet food recall, I've seen many more—and more than a few of them made that change with help and support from Lew.

Her book is an invaluable tool for making that switch in your own dog's life, or addressing specific dietary needs due to changing age, health, or lifestyle. It occupies that rational middle ground between "pet food is so complicated no one can possibly feed their dog without a commercial laboratory and degree in biology" and "just feed your dog anything and she'll be fine."

It doesn't need to take an international food safety crisis to know why and how to make your dog's food yourself. It only takes common sense and basic information, both of which you'll find in abundance in this book.

Christie Keith
San Francisco, California

Part I
Nutrition Basics

Chapter One

The Untold History of Dog Food

There is probably no more enduring symbol of wordless, unbreakable friendship than of man and his dog. It is a union that has lasted since dogs first became our companions, crossing borders and transcending cultural differences. In our hectic modern lives, when so many things have changed, it is comforting to know that some things remain the same. Dogs are still our best friends; they will never be upgraded, outdated, or replaced. They are our companions and guides, our workers and soul mates. In some ways they still remain a mystery. We know how to walk them, how to bathe them, and how to recognize when they smile. However, many of us become baffled when it comes to decisions about what or how to feed them.

A walk through any modern grocery store shows how obsessed we have become with our own health and endless dietary possibilities, yet how much do we really know about the dietary needs of our dogs?

The choice of commercial dog food for our pets is in many ways confusing. So many of us don't know what dogs really need in their diet, and commercial pet foods are filled with promises that their products have everything a dog should need. If we look behind the colorful labels and clever ads of the pet food companies, we see an industry far more concerned with sales and marketing than with what they are selling: products high in carbohydrates, fiber, and fillers along with low-quality proteins.

> How much do we really know about the dietary needs of our greatest friends?

Pet food is a huge industry these days by any measure. *Business Week* estimates that we spend $41 billion annually on our cats and dogs, more than half of that on food and medicines.[1] With such financial power and with the support of many veterinarians, the pet food industry has come to control not only what our pets eat, but a lot of what we think we know about their anatomy and their nutritional needs.

Those of us who grew up with commercial pet food—including seeing pet food ads on television, shopping for pet food in dedicated aisles in the supermarket, and enjoying the ease of feeding instant food to our dogs—can scarcely imagine a time without processed dog food. "Dog food" has become less a term for what we feed our pets than a way of thinking about canine nutrition. It has become so easy to pull a can off the shelf that we don't even think about what our pet's dietary needs are. We trust the pet food companies to make these decisions for us. Many of us simply think commercial dog foods are just heavily processed "people food," specifically made for shelf-life and economy, that they promote a healthy animal.

> "Dog food" has become less a term for what we feed our pets than a way of thinking about canine nutrition.

Surprisingly enough, despite their availability around the world today, dog foods are a relatively recent invention. Though the first commercial dog food appeared in the 19th century, the use of bagged and canned foods only became popular in the United States after World War II. Before that time dogs simply ate whatever they could find in their environment (with a little help from their friends, of course). For farm dogs this meant raw meat scraps, raw milk, eggs, and food found by scavenging. City dogs usually depended on scraps from their owners' tables with some offal and cheap cuts of raw meat from the butcher. Only the dogs of royalty and the very rich had carefully prepared diets.

In 1860 a man named James Spratt came upon some dogs at a shipyard. They were scavenging "hardtack" that they had been thrown from navy ships by sailors in port. This gave him the inspiration and motivation for a new idea. With the help of his partner, Charles Cruft, dog food as we know it was born. Spratt, perhaps not completely aware of the marketing possibilities of his new creations, called them "Spratt's Patent Meat Fibrine Dog Cakes." While the name wasn't catchy, his marketing strategy was pure genius. Spratt began holding dog shows to market his products.[2] His biscuits were not complicated, but made of just a few simple and readily available ingredients. Soon other companies jumped on the bandwagon. Some employed veterinarians to endorse their products, claiming their foods could cure dogs of worms and other common ailments, a marketing trend that continues today.[3]

Perhaps the most successful marketing ploy was the simplest one in that it appealed to the public's bottom line. As the economy collapsed during the 1930s, pet food began to be marketed as a cheaper alternative to home cooking. Sales began to pick up. Capitalizing on this bright idea, the pet food industry came up with two cheap, convenient inventions that are now the mainstays of dog food even today. They were canned meat and dehydrated dog food, both introduced into American dog bowls in the 1940s. "Just add water," the instructions stated, and dinner was served.[4]

As competition heated up between rival companies, debate emerged on the benefits of their formulas. Each company praised the virtues of processed, mass-produced food, some saying that they were able to utilize waste products such as grain hulls, sweepings, and meat unusable for human consumption; others that fresh meat was just too expensive to feed dogs and that such foods made them too "finicky." While it was generally acknowledged that fresh meat and vegetables were superior, the companies argued that dogs could be fed more economically with these factory waste products and still do well. It wasn't until a few decades later that the companies became bold enough to say that your dog actually *required* these waste products for good health. At the time the combination of saving money and convenience was powerful enough.

As dog food sales continued to gather pace after World War II, dog food was considered to be a win-win situation for everyone. Mill operators and grain dealers found a lucrative market for their by-products; slaughterhouses were able to sell non-human grade meat, unusable parts, and by-products. At the end of the chain, consumers found an easy, cheap way to feed their pets. Companies grew larger from the growing demand. Suddenly food that had always been discarded found its way into the dinner bowls of dogs all over America.[5]

What was lost in the rush to grow the industry and satisfy consumers was an awareness of what the dogs were actually eating. Since many of the meat sources in dog food were non-human grade, it became common to combine these with grains and cook them for days to kill bacteria and disease. This process, which has been the standard in the industry almost since the beginning, has repeatedly failed, producing food with unwanted contaminants and creating the need for recalls. Furthermore, studies show that such prolonged exposure to high temperatures destroys or seriously damages many of the nutrients that go into the mixture at the beginning.[6]

To offset consumers' doubts, the pet food industry had ample responses in the form of new technologies they touted as improving the process and the product. In the 1950s the Purina Company, which is still going strong today, made a breakthrough they called "extrusion," a process in which the ingredients were combined and cooked together in liquid form before being expanded and baked. The resulting pieces were much larger and lighter than the pellets; the companies began to market them to the public as a cost-effective alternative to the kibble products already on the market. This gimmick, like Spratt's dog shows a hundred years earlier, was another in a long line of clever promotions for commercial dog food.[7]

The pet food companies' message? Table scraps, a canine staple for as long as anyone could remember, were harmful. To be safe, they said, you *had* to feed your dog processed food.

In the 1960s the competition for food sales heated up, as the pet food industry stepped up the use of veterinarians to proclaim that all the currently available meat-based dog foods were incomplete.[8] This set the tone for canine nutrition that still holds influence today. The editor of the *Journal of the American Veterinary Medical Association*, in agreeing with the pet food industry's views, stated that dog foods needed to be fortified with nutrients, that too much protein was harmful, and that some carbohydrates were necessary for a dog's health. The Pet Food Institute, the mouthpiece of the pet food industry, drove the message home with an extraordinary press offensive that included articles in major American magazines, airtime on ninety-one radio stations, and press releases sent out to a thousand newspapers. Their message was that table scraps, a canine staple for as long as anyone could remember, were harmful. To be safe, they said, you *had* to feed your dog processed food.[9]

Convenience remained the biggest attraction of prepared and packaged dog foods in that scooping dry pieces of food into the dog's food bowl was much easier than cooking and preparing your pet's dinner. The developments in dog food were just keeping pace with all the other advancements in modern technology that were developed to make our lives "easier." It seemed like a logical progression. People still had some concerns about their dog's health and the food they were eating. So the dog food companies, on the back of the announcement that existing foods were incomplete, began labeling their dog foods as "complete" and advertised that no additional foods or supplements were necessary. They echoed the Pet Food Institute's warnings that adding table scraps could actually be dangerous to a dog's health. No longer was pet food simply an efficient use of slaughterhouse and grain mill waste products that your dogs could eat as an item of convenience. It was now promoted as what they needed to survive.

Marketing continued to evolve over the coming decades as celebrities were recruited to endorse particular brands and more and more gimmicks and cosmetic strategies were employed to attract the animals and their owners. Suddenly there were dog foods that could produce their own gravy, kibble cut into shapes that were compelling to the dog owner, and dyes in the dog food to make it look "natural." A kind of artistry began to develop as foods came to be designed more to meet owners' aesthetic idea of an appetizing meal than to support dogs' health. Pet food sales moved from the feed stores to the supermarkets, with bright labels, appealing pictures, and promises of health and well-being. The marketing strategies paid off as dog food sales continued to skyrocket.

As their monopoly on canine nutrition became established, the pet food companies moved on to specialty diets formulated for specific diseases or disorders in pets. From the first diet developed for kidney and heart disease in 1948, the niche has grown to include more than twenty specialty diets today. Dr. Mark Morris DVM, founder of Hill's Pet Products and Science Diet, was the first of many to develop specialty diets. But what made his products so popular was not their specific recipes, but their point of sale. Only veterinarians offered these prescription diets. This new, more scientific approach to marketing dog food began to portray dog nutrition as a complex issue, one that the public couldn't be trusted to understand for themselves. People came to rely more on the labels' advice about nutrition than their own judgment and common sense. As time went on, the dog food aisle of the supermarket expanded to include the veterinarian's office.

Until 1974 the National Research Council (NRC) was responsible for developing the protocol for the nutritional values needed in pet food. In the mid 1970s[10] the pet food purveyors, now a giant industry, set up a new organization called the American Association of Feed Control Officials (AAFCO). AAFCO quickly set about changing the NRC's testing procedures by shortening the testing periods and making them less rigorous. Soon the existing extended feeding trials of dog food were used less often and replaced by a simple chemical analysis of the food. While this provided figures for the dog food, they were all but meaningless—these "figures" gave no hint as to the type of food used, its freshness, or the digestibility of each of the ingredients. As the Animal Protection Institute (API) wrote at the time, this left the pet food industry to police itself without the worry of government intervention.[11]

In 1985 the NRC updated their guidelines for nutrition, making several important changes aimed at finding more accurate ways of listing how nutritious dog food really was after it had been combined, cooked, and processed,[12] so that owners could be sure that the figures they were seeing were a true reflection of what they were buying.[13]

No serious efforts have been made to even list the food ingredients based on how easily a dog can digest them.

How did the pet food companies respond? Ben Sheffy from the James A. Baker Institute for Animal Health at Cornell University participated in the 1985 NRC revision. The responses, he said, ranged from "disappointment to anger." To date, no serious efforts have been made to implement the NRC's 1985 proposed changes or to even list the food ingredients based on how easily a dog can digest them.[14]

Without the annoyance of regulatory interference, the pet food industry continued doing what it does best, finding new ways to market the same food. Their next invention was "premium" dog food, advertised to be more nutritious for dogs. Many dog owners began to ask this question: if the premium foods are only appearing now, then what have I been feeding my dog all these years? They needn't have worried, since most of the "premium" foods relied on old recipes using the outdated NRC 1974 standards. The "premium" banner, as the specialty diets before it, allowed the pet food industry to expand their product ranges into the variety seen on shelves today, including diets for puppies, senior dogs, maintenance, and performance. The public became more confused—not only could they not be trusted to feed an adult dog, now different formulas were "needed" at each stage of the dog's life.

The "new and improved" approach to marketing that was so favored by pet food companies became well worn by the 1980s. While the public was kept out of the loop of canine nutrition, each "advance" in diet and nutrition gave the public the impression that the science was simply developing with the times and that they had to keep up. The trend continues today in a market that is saturated with products displayed with claims of scientifically proven formulas and specific "complete" diets.

The industry continues to go to great lengths to ensure veterinarians endorse their products. They believe veterinarians lend an air of authenticity and integrity to their claims that mere advertising can't accomplish on its own. Veterinarians today continue to encourage the use of dry dog foods and instill a fear in pet owners about preparing meals for their own dogs. A brief glance at the Canadian Veterinarian Association pamphlet on pet food, *A Commonsense Guide to Feeding Your Dog or Cat,* is more or less up front about saying dog owners shouldn't be responsible for preparing their own pet's food. "Homemade diets are not recommended," it says, "because there is a good chance that all the necessary nutrients will not be provided. Incorrect preparation and cooking may also deplete certain nutrients and result in a deficient diet. As well, homemade diets are usually more expensive to produce, without providing better nutrition."[15]

Interestingly, the same authority responsible for this pamphlet also runs the pet food certification system in Canada. They tell us canine nutrition is a mysterious affair best left to researchers, scientists, veterinarians, and, of course, the pet food industry. The Pet Food Institute is the mouthpiece of the Pet Food Industry. The Pet Food Institute represents more than ninety-five percent of all cat and dog food companies in the United States. According to their advice, it is of great importance that your pet's health be left up to the companies it represents.

Under "Pet Nutrition" on the Pet Food Institute's website, they tell us, "with today's wide assortment of commercial pet foods fully formulated for all stages of pet growth, it is easy to feed your pet well-balanced meals." Predictably they warn against feeding your pets yourself, saying, "Veterinarians and animal nutritionists have determined that table scraps are not balanced meals for pets and are deficient in nutrients. Supervise your pet's diet carefully ... make sure the food you use is specifically labeled 'complete and balanced.'"[16]

Toward the end of the 1980s, as consumers became more educated about—and in some cases, even obsessed by—their own nutrition, it became common practice to read the labels on food products. It didn't take long before the public began taking more notice of some strange-sounding ingredients in their pets' food. Soon enough dog owners began asking questions about what they were feeding their dogs, seeking answers from the pet food companies about the chemical preservatives and the quality of the meat found in most processed dog foods.

After sustained public pressure concerning their use of these chemicals, many pet food companies have eliminated them and are now using vitamin C and vitamin E to preserve fat in dog food. Ever inventive, the pet food companies allowed necessity to mother another clever invention. The current trend in commercial dog foods is "natural" foods, whereby companies now offer organic or human-grade foods along with new forms of meat, like venison, fish, or rabbit. Some even offer whole chickens as the main meat ingredient and claim they don't use meat by-products or other less nutritious ingredients. What they don't advertise is that all the brands still continue to heavily process and cook all the ingredients as they have always done; nor do they tell us that the food is still predominately grains, grain fillers, starches, vegetables, fibers, and grain by-products.

> What they don't advertise is that all the brands still continue to heavily process and cook all the ingredients as they have always done.

There have been some questions from the public on pet food ingredients. Recent years have seen several challenges to the traditional authority of the pet food industry. In the early 1990s a group of Australian vets began to rebel against the pet food industry and openly claimed that processed dog food was responsible for most of the ailments they treated, from dental problems to cancer.[17] In 2007 toxic wheat gluten from China made headlines after it was found to have caused the deaths of hundreds, possibly thousands, of pets. People have begun to ask more questions about the food they feed their animals and what their pets really need. With the increasing influence of the Internet, pet owners are finding they are able to come together as a community to share ideas and negate some of the influence of the pet food companies and veterinary community in ways that weren't possible previously.

Many consumers are now more aware of the ingredients in commercial dog food, most notably the sources of protein and the high percentages of grain. Many know that most processed dog foods are a kind of junk food made of waste products and cooked for days on end. However, this growing awareness has not changed the relationship between the pet food industry and veterinarians. The pet food industry continues to write and publish pet nutrition textbooks for veterinary colleges. Aspiring vets are taught to tell their clients that only processed dog foods are scientifically proven to meet their dogs' nutritional needs. One could only imagine the uproar if a similar system was in place for the human medical system, in which doctors were taught to convince people that processed food was not only beneficial, but absolutely necessary.

Dog owners who want to learn more about canine nutrition and feeding their dogs a fresh-food diet will find only a handful of books on the subject. Very few veterinarians will encourage home-cooked or raw diets for dogs. Hopefully by reading this book and following the recipes, you can understand how simple, inexpensive, and satisfying it is to keep your dog happy and healthy.

Chapter Two

Canine Digestion and Anatomy Made Simple

House Dogs and Wild Carnivores

Examining a dog's sharp, jagged teeth shows you how dogs and their ancestors evolved, as carnivores, able to tear through flesh and fat easily. Canines have no flat molars to grind vegetable matter. While the teeth are easy to see, other parts of a dog's anatomy, such as the digestive system, have remained a little more mysterious and caused a lot of debate among dog lovers.

In recent times as we have come to learn more about our own bodies, people have begun to ask more questions about their canine friends. Are they carnivores or omnivores? Do they need carbohydrates? Can homemade diets satisfy their needs?

With the confusing and compromised information available from the pet food industry and their veterinarian counterparts, it can make your dog's digestion and anatomy seem like a complex and difficult issue. What it comes down to is just learning a few simple guidelines that govern dogs' bodies, and then adjusting how you feed and care for your dog accordingly. Before you know it you'll be well on your way to helping your dog to live a long and healthy life.

Dogs, like their ancient wolf ancestors, are designed to eat meat. Wolves are members of the carnivore family known as *Canis lupus*. The domestic dog is also of the carnivore family, known as *Canis familiaris*. In his book *The Carnivores*, R. F. Ewer (lecturer in biology at the University of Ghana) states that "*Canis familiaris* is generally believed to have evolved from the wolf, the wild species that it most closely resembles both anatomically and

> Canine digestion and anatomy may seem complex; in fact they are simpler than our own.

behaviorally. The differences between the two are not great enough to make it necessary to postulate a hypothetical ancestral wild species which has neither survived to the present day nor left any known fossil remains."

Carnivores are built with the shortest and simplest digestive tracts of all mammals, allowing them to easily digest animal protein and fat. Their jaws are hinged to open wide so they can swallow large chunks of meat whole, allowing them to gorge on large quantities of food at one time and then rest until the next meal. Those same jaws are not designed to do the sideways grinding needed to fully pulverize grains and vegetables in order to digest these foods properly.

So while our dogs may no longer be hunting in packs and bringing down big game, their bodies are still the same and they still have the same nutritional needs.

Figure 2.1. Digestion Anatomy Types in Mammals.			
Digestive Type	Carnivore	Omnivore	Herbivore
Digestive Tract	Short	Medium	Long
Teeth	Sharp, jagged, blade-shaped	Flat molars and sharp teeth	Strong, flat molars
Primary food	Meat	Meat and vegetation	Vegetation

Rule #1: Animal Protein

So what does your dog need to live a long and happy life? The short answer is animal protein. Animal proteins contain all the essential amino acids dogs need for a strong body, a healthy coat, and good digestion. With their short and simple digestive tracts, dogs can't ferment and digest vegetables and grains like herbivores and omnivores. They are able to make quick work of meat and fat and thrive on it. (See "Chapter Three: Protein Is a Dog's Best Friend.")

Industrial Strength Stomach

Dogs digest food differently than omnivores and herbivores. Their digestive tract is shorter and simpler and the stomach does a great job of breaking down fat, protein, and bones. This is accomplished by the strong hydrochloric acid in the dog's stomach, which can break down harmful bacteria and fully digest animal proteins, bones, and fat.

Dogs are able to eat all kinds of things we humans can't digest well at all. Pet health and nutrition experts Steve Brown and Beth Taylor write in their book *See Spot Live Longer* that the "industrial strength" hydrochloric acid in dogs' stomachs "can dissolve iron."[18] So it is no surprise, then, that an old steak that would leave you seriously ill is just a delicious dinner for your dog. Dogs can keep food in their stomachs (where they are kept in an acidic condition) for up to eight hours and pass small amounts of digested material through the small intestine quickly. The canine digestive tract is developed to kill germs and stop them from multiplying. Humans, in contrast, let food pass through into the intestines in as little as thirty to sixty minutes, but the food can remain in the small intestines from twelve to sixty hours, creating a better chance for germs to multiply and cause problems.

Dogs' digestive process provides them protection for consuming prey, drinking pond water, and eating food contaminated with bacteria. Bacteria like salmonella, *E. Coli,* and other food-borne pathogens are not such a problem for dogs and are usually dealt with during the extended time in the powerfully acidic environment of the stomach and rapid pass through the small intestine.

So Why All the Carbohydrates?

Most dog food recipes are based upon the premise that the digestive system of the dog is similar to humans and that they need carbohydrates for energy and digestion. This logic has been so pervasive that most homemade dog recipes are usually not much different from those used by the commercial brands, following the same ratio of animal protein, carbohydrates and fat. The main reason carbohydrates are so common in commercial dog food is most likely cost. Grains are much cheaper to add to processed dog food than meat, and have a longer shelf life. Chapter 4 will discuss the need to reduce carbohydrates in the diet. For some conditions, carbohydrates may be needed, but for the most part they can be eliminated or kept to twenty-five percent or less of the diet. (See "Chapter Four:The Real Low-Carb Revolution.")

What, No Vegetables?

With all the focus over the last decade on eating your fruits and vegetables, not to mention the campaigns against meat, it can be difficult to re-orient yourself to the fact that dogs just can't make use of the same foods that are so instrumental in keeping us healthy. Some of the things we know about human nutrition hold true for dogs (raw, unprocessed, fresh food is good for them) but some things are completely different (they need animal protein and fat, and can't make much use of vegetables).

Like their ancient wolf ancestors, dogs are not designed to digest foods that need fermenting or further breaking down. Their bodies are designed for animal proteins and fat. These are thoroughly digested in the stomach and then proceed to the small intestine. There the essential amino acids are removed and broken down from the protein and the lipids from the fat. Additions of significant amounts of plant materials like grains, vegetables, fruit, and fiber simply cause gas and large, smelly stools. A few vegetables in the diet are acceptable, but they should only form a small part of their diet, ideally no more than twenty-five percent for most dogs. (See "Part II: Feeding Your Dog the Easy Way" for recipes and more information on feeding your pet.)

Chapter Three

Protein Is a Dog's Best Friend

Protein: Your Dog's Superfood

Since dogs are carnivores with digestive systems designed to handle large amounts of raw meat and fat, it makes sense that they would thrive on the diet nature intended.

Protein is the staple of the carnivore and an important element in your dog's diet. It is essential for good tissue health, a strong immune system, and a healthy coat and skin. Recent studies have confirmed that a high level of protein is not just beneficial, but necessary for dogs of all ages from growing puppies to senior dogs. So just what is protein and how do dogs get what they need?

When people think of proteins, they usually think of meat, fish, eggs, and dairy. All of these are good sources of protein. Grains and vegetables also contain proteins, however when it comes to dogs, not all proteins are created equal.

Amino Acids

Proteins are made up of groups of amino acids and these amino acids come in two types: the essential and the non-essential. Even if your dog doesn't receive enough non-essential amino acids from dietary sources, his or her body can synthesize them well enough. Essential amino acids need to be present in the dog's meals in the right amounts for the diet to be truly "balanced and complete."

A look at a list of all the amino acids, with their long scientific names might be enough to convince you of the old myth that canine nutrition really *is* a complex issue! But you don't need to know the names of all of them, nor do you even need to know in what amounts your dog needs them. Why? Because they are all found, in the correct amounts, in the simple staple foods that should make up the basis of your dog's diet. (See "In a Nutshell" for a list of all the amino acids. See "Part II: Feeding Your Dog the Easy Way" for more information on feeding your dog.)

Not All Proteins Are Created Equal

The quality of a protein is determined by how many of these essential amino acids it contains. The more amino acids a protein includes, the more digestible or "available" it is for your dog. Animal proteins that contain all the amino acids are considered "complete" proteins. Plant proteins are considered "incomplete" because they are missing l-carnitine and taurine.

The yardstick for measuring protein quality is the chicken egg, which is considered to have the all of the amino acids your dog needs.

Figure 3.1. Comparison of Proteins.*
Protein Digestibility
Egg whites: 1.00
Muscle meats (chicken, beef, lamb): 0.92
Organ meats (kidney, liver): 0.90
Milk, cheese: 0.89
Fish: 0.78
Rice: 0.72
Oats: 0.66
Wheat: 0.64
Corn: 0.54

* Note: Values in this table are approximate, as they have been taken from several nutritional sources and personal communications with nutrition experts.

The next best thing to eggs is protein from animal meat and organs. Plant proteins on the other end of the scale can fall as low as forty-five percent on the digestibility scale.

This is when the problem with feeding plant proteins to your dog lies: even if you feed your dog twice as many plant proteins as you would animal proteins, they still wouldn't get all the amino acids needed. Quantity unfortunately is no substitute for quality.

The best choice is to feed your dog animal protein. And just as a meal prepared at home beats a fast food meal for providing the nutrients we need, there are a number of things that can affect the quality and digestibility of meats and their amino acids.

The human raw food movement was founded on the understanding that cooking destroys nutrients and enzymes in food and alters their make-up, usually for the worse. Similarly, studies have shown that high temperatures and prolonged exposure to heat can alter amino acid chains, making the essential amino acids less available and digestible to dogs. At worst, the protein is destroyed; at the very least the quality of the protein suffers. It seems the longer you cook proteins, the less useful they become.[19]

While prolonged or high-temperature cooking may be necessary for omnivores—how many of us would eat a raw steak each night?—carnivores have digestive tracts designed to readily and easily digest raw meat.

As we have already learned, canned and dry dog foods tend to be overcooked and high in fiber which makes them hard for dogs to digest. And if you take a quick look at the quality of the ingredients going into them at the beginning, not to mention the cooking process, it is not difficult to see that the protein quality in most processed dog foods is questionable at best.

This brings us to the same problem some owners have with plant protein. You can feed your dog as much low-quality protein as you like, but it still won't meet their needs. Not only will it not satisfy your dog nutritionally, but it can create a whole host of other problems as well. Poor quality proteins are more taxing on your dog's liver and kidneys and over time can cause deficiencies that may compromise even the healthiest dog's organs. Some dog owners tend to over-feed their pets to try to make up for the lack of quality in the processed food through sheer quantity. This can lead to obesity and other serious health complications.

Your dog needs regular meals of fresh, good-quality protein. This doesn't always mean shopping for food in the meat aisle of your local supermarket. There are many creative and cost-effective ways to help your dog get the nutrition he or she needs.

Protein and Organ Health

The common wisdom for feeding has been to limit protein for puppies, older dogs, and dogs with kidney and liver problems. However science does not support this approach.

Dr. D. S. Kronfeld, who conducted a number of pioneering studies on canine nutrition, dispelled this myth, finding that older dogs and dogs with compromised kidneys can easily digest high-quality proteins. He found older dogs actually thrive on high-quality protein. If given in high enough doses these proteins kill bacteria in the kidneys and create an acidic condition that promotes organ health, fighting off infections and bacteria in the dogs' systems.[20] A study was performed in which dogs with only one kidney were tested over a number of years. It was found that a diet high in protein did not hurt the dogs at all, but instead increased their chances of survival.[21]

Protein and Seniors

A diet rich in protein is especially important for older dogs. Senior dogs are less efficient at making use of protein so they need more of it to help compensate. Research has shown that healthy older dogs may need as much as fifty percent more protein than healthy young adult dogs.[22] Other studies have shown older dogs fed high-protein diets over several years maintain more lean body mass and less fat than those fed the recommended lower amounts.[23] (See "Chapter Thirteen: Feeding Senior Dogs" for more detail on how to feed your older dog.)

Protein and Puppies

Puppies, like their parents, always need high-quality protein to grow up healthy and strong. Too little protein will do more harm than good. There is no evidence to show that too much protein is damaging to a growing puppy. We will learn more about how to take care of their dietary needs in upcoming chapters. (See "Chapter Twelve: Feeding Your Puppy" for more information on protein and puppies and on feeding your puppy.)

So What Should I Feed Then?

The best complete protein choices include:

- Red meat
- Poultry
- Organ meat
- Cultured dairy (yogurt, cottage cheese)
- Eggs

Always remember that no single choice will offer the variety needed for good health. A dog needs a balance of these different proteins to achieve optimal health. And while plant proteins offer fiber and some minerals and vitamins, only animal-based proteins will give the full array of amino acids needed for your dog's good health and longevity. Additionally, dogs need not just protein, but also calcium, fat, and some fiber to create a well-rounded diet. We will discuss how to balance your dog's meals in "Part II: Feeding Your Dog the Easy Way," which includes recipes.

In a Nutshell

Five rules for feeding your dog protein:

1. Never use too little.
2. Always use complete animal proteins.
3. Plant proteins are no substitute for animal proteins.
4. Avoid using low-quality protein.
5. It is necessary to add calcium when feeding protein in supplement form *unless* you are including raw meaty bones in your dog's meals (more on that later).

Good quality animal protein is the single best thing you can feed your dog. Feeding your dog a variety of complete animal proteins ensures that a wide spectrum of amino acids are being provided and will keep your dog happy and satisfied at meal time. (For more information on the use of meat in canine diets, see "Chapter Seventeen: Why Your Dog Is Not a Vegetarian.")

Figure 3.2. Essential Amino Acids.		
Arginine	Lysine	Threonine
Histidine	Methionine	Typotophan
Isolueucine	Phenylalanine	Valine
Leucine	Taurine	

Figure 3.3. Nonessential Amino Acids.		
Alanine	Glutamate	Lycine
Asparagine	Glutamine	Proline
Aspartate	Glycine	Serine
Carnitine	Hydroxlysine	Tyrosine
Cysteine	Hydroxyproline	

Chapter Four

The Real Low-Carb Revolution

Low Carbs or No Carbs?

Walking into any supermarket these days, it is hard not to notice the vast array of products sporting "low-carb" labels. It is a shame that when you reach the dog food aisle they are nowhere to be seen. It is the one place where they are needed.

The starches and cellulose in grains and carbohydrates are useful for herbivores and humans. Without them we would find it hard to digest and eliminate anything we eat. With dogs it is a much different matter.

Since dogs don't have the flat grinding teeth, a long digestive tract, or amylase in their saliva, they have a difficult time with diets high in complex carbohydrates. Carbohydrates tend to stay in dogs' digestive tract longer, which slows down the digestive process and can cause spasms and irritations in the large intestine as the dog must labor to process them.[24]

We have learned that dogs lack the digestive system for converting carbohydrates into a form they can utilize. Symptoms of a diet too high in starches can range from bulky, smelly stools to dehydration, gas, and irritable bowel syndrome. In the long term, too many carbohydrates can dramatically reduce your dog's quality of life and may result in health complications.

Many of us have seen the telltale stool of a dog who eats too many carbohydrates—it is too big, contains too much moisture, and smells terrible. It is the dog's way of telling you that his or her digestion is under stress.

> Carbohydrates are found in everything from honey to milk, but we most often think of them in terms of grains and vegetables.

The National Research Council (NRC), which sets the nutritional standards for dog food, does not list a carbohydrate requirement. They do include a long list of amino acids, along with fat and some specific minerals, all of which can be found in abundance in the animal protein sources that should be the staple of any healthy dog's diet. These include meat, bones, organ meat, dairy, and eggs.

What's in Your Dog Food

Canine nutrition textbooks tell us that most commercial dog foods consist of sixty percent carbohydrates like bran, beet pulp, rice and peanut hulls, cellulose, and plant gums, which dogs have difficulty digesting. (Dry dog foods are composed mainly of cereal or starches, which are largely made up of corn, wheat, potatoes, rice, and sometimes soy.)[25] It is common practice to use a large quantity of grains in commercial dog food. But is there any science behind this practice? Reading canine nutrition textbooks can be more confusing than illuminating.

Carbohydrates are often listed in canine nutrition books as an essential part of the diet, yet nowhere do they mention how much a dog needs. In fact, they seem to be quite confused on the subject. From a 1978 article on feeding dogs, "carbohydrate is physiologically essential to the dog and cat; however it is not essential in the diet."[26] (We can only gather from this mysterious explanation that carbohydrates, like non-essential amino acids, can be synthesized by the dogs themselves.) The same article confuses the issue further, saying, "the fact that dogs and cats do not require carbohydrates in the diets is usually immaterial because the nutrient content of most commercial foods includes at least a moderate level of this nutrient." What strange logic. Your dog doesn't need this stuff, it seems to say, but it is there anyway, so that doesn't matter.[27]

While dog food companies would have you believe that grains are a good source of protein, the fact is that dogs just don't have the anatomy to digest and make use of protein from carbohydrates.

Dog food companies say they use high-fiber carbohydrates to help dogs with digestion. But if they really wanted to offer nutritious fiber, why wouldn't they use something like pulped vegetables, which can offer your dog some level of nutrition? Of course, as with high-quality animal proteins, pulped vegetables wouldn't maintain their integrity through the long and intense processing that commercial food goes through. By the time dry and canned dog foods are processed, dog food manufacturers need to add nutrients to meet nutritional standards.

Cameron's Story

Cameron was one and a half years old when she was put into rescue. She had been suffering from the debilitating skin condition *active demodex* since she was three months old and had been turned into a rural shelter to be euthanatized after the family could no longer afford her medical bills. Cameron had been in constant pain for most of her life, with raw and open sores on her face and the tops of her paws.

In combination with vet treatment, she was put on a low-to-no-carbohydrate diet, starting on grain-free kibble and treats, before transitioning to a raw diet. Since then the change has been dramatic—her skin has improved considerably and she has been scab-free for several months now. Cameron is living proof of the kind of transformation the right diet can make.

The Danger of Carbohydrates

Not only do all these carbohydrates not help your dog, they can actually be harmful. Dr. Kronfeld has pointed out that too much fiber is actually dangerous. He cites the case of racing sled dogs who were fed large amounts of fiber to keep up their energy levels and ended up suffering from bleeding bowels. Kronfeld found that fiber can also cause problems in the colon and rectum, while other studies link carbohydrates and grains to a number of health problems including arthritis, allergies, and seizures, among others.[28]

The cellulose in fiber is indigestible by dogs and the starches can decrease the absorption of calcium, magnesium, zinc, and iron. Both can cause your dog to become lethargic while hampering protein digestion.[29] Kronfeld points out that canines have been eating meat and fat for ten thousand years and fiber for only a hundred. We can only surmise then that they can function perfectly well without them.[30]

A Most Embarrassing Problem

Most of us have had the distaste of seeing our dogs eat another dog's stool. One minute you're walking along, enjoying a walk in the park, and the next thing you know, your dog is eating something you know they shouldn't. So why does it happen?

Much of the time, the problem can be traced back to carbohydrates. When dogs digest grains, reserves of important bacteria in your dog's intestines become depleted, causing essential vitamins like vitamins B and K to be passed with the feces. When your dog eats another dog's stool he or she may be trying to get back the bacteria and enzymes that are missing in his or her diet. Carbohydrates are more difficult to digest, and may pass through the dog's system only partially digested. This may also make stool more tempting to your dog.

So what can you do? As we will learn a little later, adding digestive enzymes, beneficial bacteria, and a B complex vitamin to the dog's diet may help curb his or her drive to eat stool. Reducing or eliminating carbohydrates can also produce smaller, less "appetizing" stools in which the food is more completely digested.

Feces are most often one quarter solid material and three quarters water. A diet heavy in carbohydrates like grains tends to produce larger stools with more water, which can result in dehydration. A diet of raw meat and bones, on the other hand, produces smaller, drier, and less smelly stools. The fewer grains your dog eats, the more beneficial enzymes and bacteria remain available to ensure stools are well-formed and almost odorless. It will also help ensure that your dog doesn't have to go looking for other dogs' stools to get those nutrients.

Do You Ever Need to Feed Carbohydrates?

Veterinarians will often tell you that a high-fiber diet is useful for your dog if he or she is suffering from irritable bowel syndrome or other gastric problems. But this recommendation is based more on an understanding of the human digestive system than your dog's. In fact, feeding this type of diet is more likely to cause an irritable bowel. A continuous diet of high fiber foods has the ability to keep the small intestine in constant irritation and inflammation. It may produce smaller stools, as fiber removes moisture from waste matter in the large intestine, but the underlying condition will remain. Alternatively, some experts suggest a diet that is bland, low in fiber and highly nutritious for dogs with gastric problems.[31]

Dr. Kronfeld reports that carbohydrates may be needed in two situations: puppies just coming off the mother's milk (which is twelve percent carbohydrates) and the lactating bitch, who needs three times the usual turnover of blood glucose to produce milk. In these cases, pulped vegetables are the most nutritious option. After weaning, Kronfeld says, you can do away with carbohydrates, as a dog's body is able to get everything it needs from other sources.[32]

It is often said that bitches need carbohydrates throughout pregnancy and after giving birth. Studies completed in the 1980s of pregnant and lactating bitches, however, showed that when they were fed a carbohydrate-free diet, their protein and fat levels increased and they whelped better. The dogs were still able to produce a good supply of milk, and their pups' survival rates were comparable to those of bitches fed carbohydrates.[33]

(There are a couple of other specific health conditions that require some carbohydrates, and we will learn more about them in "Part III: Remedial Diets Made Simple.")

Remember to increase protein and fat for dogs fed a carbohydrate-free diet so that gylcogenesis (conversion of fat to glucose) can occur.

Even though carbohydrates may not offer much nutritional value to a dog, adding pulped vegetables to the diet in small quantities is not harmful and may have some nutritional value. I recommend feeding vegetables and/or grains at a ratio of less than one sixth of a raw diet, and about one quarter of a home-cooked diet. Remember that using fiber in larger quantities than this increases stool bulk and may require more of your dog's energy to digest, so be wary of including too much.

What about Energy?

The last argument for using grains in dog foods is that carbohydrates are an energy source. Many canine nutrition books tell us that the glucose found in grains is necessary for stamina, endurance, and performance. Unlike humans, dogs can convert fat to glucose in the liver if given in high enough doses. Dogs fed a high level of protein (fifty percent) and fat can easily manage this, making proteins and fats, not carbohydrates, the key to keeping your dog full of energy.

Chapter Five

Fats for Canine Health

So Much Fat?

With the modern obsession with weight and dieting, it can be difficult to accept what is one of the most fundamental truths of canine nutrition—your dog needs fats and lots of them. Fats:

- Are necessary for the absorption of fat-soluble vitamins;
- Provide protection from the cold;
- Protect the nerve fibers in the body;
- Provide more calories per gram than carbohydrates or protein;
- Improve the flavor and palatability of the dog's food;
- Help satiate the appetite;
- Are an excellent source of essential fatty acids.

If we want to help our dogs stay strong and healthy we really have to start thinking differently about fats. Fats don't affect canines in the same way as humans when it comes to issues of cholesterol or heart disease. Because of their different anatomy as carnivores, dogs don't run the same risk of cholesterol clogging the arteries or causing strokes.*

What Kinds of Fat?

Animal fats are the best for your dog. These would include whole milk yogurt, canned fish, meat, and fish oils.

---

* High cholesterol can indicate certain problems, such as hypothyroidism, cushing's disease, or diabetes. If your pet tests high for cholesterol, always have your veterinarian check for these health problems.

It is important that fats fed to dogs are fresh. Dogs may have strong stomachs and powerful tools for digesting fat, but rancid and poor-quality fats can still do them harm. In some cases they can rob them of essential fatty acids, the beneficial fats they need to stay healthy. Equally important is making sure your dog gets enough fat in the diet. A fat-deficient diet can affect the coat and skin, giving rise to conditions like pruritis (itching), dermatitis (skin inflammation), and seborrhea.

Fatty Acids

Fatty acids form an essential part of your dog's diet. The two most important fatty acids for your dog are omega-6 and omega-3, both of which have found some level of popularity in human diets in recent times. And it is no wonder—their benefits to both people and our pets are immense.

In dogs fatty acids help control inflammation, aid in the prevention of heart disease and assist with the treatment of cancer, arthritis, orthopedic problems, and renal disease. The anti-inflammatory properties have also been found to help with dermatitis and other skin conditions, as well fighting certain gastrointestinal disorders such as inflammatory bowel disease and colitis. So where do you find these fatty acids?

Omega-6 fatty acids are found in animal sources like chicken and pork and in lesser amounts in beef. Although the best sources of omega-6 are plant sources—olive, safflower, and other plant oils—your dog should get all that is needed from meats and fats. You should never need to add omega-6 fatty acids. Omega-3 fatty acids, on the other hand, are less common and will need to be added to your dog's diet. They can be found in fish oil and to a lesser degree in marine sources like spirulina and blue green algae.[34] Cod liver oil is not the same as fish oil. Cod liver oil offers less omega-3 fatty acids and is high in vitamins A and D, which are not recommended for dogs with certain conditions such as kidney issues and pregnancy. Use regular fish oil (such as EPA fish oil and salmon oil) for omega-3 fatty acids.

Some plant-based oils, such as flax seed oil and hemp oil, do contain omega-3 fatty acids, but they are in the form of alpha-linolenic acid (ALA). Current studies have shown that dogs have difficulty converting ALA to a usable form of omega-3 fatty acids. Please remember it is best to use animal-based oils, such as fish oil or salmon oil, as a source of omega-3 fatty acids for our canine friends.[35]

Research is still incomplete on the optimal balance of omega-6 to omega-3 fatty acids in a dog's diet, but it is thought to be somewhere between 5:1 and 10:1. Too much omega-6 to omega-3 can cause problems with a dog's coat, as well as inflammation, allergies, and skin conditions.

Figure 5.1. Omega Acids.[36]		
	Omega-3 Fatty Acids	Omega-6 Fatty Acids
Found in	Fish body oils (such as fish oil and salmon oil), spirulina, blue-green algae	Chicken, pork, beef; olive, safflower, and plant oils
Supplement?	Yes	No
Balance	Between 5:1 and 10:1 Omega-6:Omega-3	

The best sources of omega-3 fatty acids are fish and salmon oils, both of which your dog can easily convert into a usable form because they contain readily available forms of omega-3 called EPA and DHA. Most plant oils have omega-3s in a form that requires further conversion, something dogs (and many people) are unable to do.

Because of the fragility of omega-3 oils (they lose their potency when they come into contact with light or oxygen, and when processed into powders) gel capsules are best.

Providing your dog with vitamin E helps to maximize his or her absorption of these acids.[37]

Putting Your Dog on a Weight-Loss Diet

When a dog gets too fat we tend to follow the human weight-control model and put him or her on a low-fat diet, usually with a low-fat, high fiber commercial dog food. Without fat, which satiates the dog's

Dog Can't Handle Fats?

Signs of a dog not digesting fat properly can range from big, foul-smelling stools, to diarrhea and dehydration. The stool is often loose and light in color, and can contain a lot of mucus. This most often occurs with cooked fats, or fats found in prepared dog foods that can sometimes go rancid if packaged too long. There can be a number of more serious reasons for your dog not digesting fats properly, the most common being liver disease, pancreatitis (inflammation or disease of the pancreas), cushing's disease, and diabetes. If supplementation and a change in diet don't help, see your veterinarian.

appetite and provides energy, your dog just gets hungry and tired. Fiber adds calories, but robs energy as the dog struggles to digest high fiber meals. If your dog needs to lose weight, just feed him or her less food. Generally, reducing the diet by about ten percent in an otherwise healthy dog is adequate.

In a Nutshell

There are three things you have to make sure of when feeding your dog fats:

1. Always include fresh fat sources in your dog's diet, including animal fat (whole milk yogurt, canned fish, meat, and eggs) and fish or salmon oil capsules.
2. Don't reduce the fat in your dog's diet if they need to lose weight. Just feed less food!
3. If your dog is having a reaction to fat (such as loose stools or stools with a strong odor), it might just mean you need to reduce the amount of fat or food you're providing. If it persists, though, it can indicate more serious health issues, so check with your vet.

Fat is essential for your dog's energy, skin, and coat, and especially for heart and kidney health. It also keeps inflammation in the joints at bay. Remember—fat is not your dog's enemy, but a very important friend!

Chapter Six

Getting the Mineral Balance Right

Making Minerals Simple

Like us, dogs need a number of minerals to stay strong and healthy. With our own bodies, it can sometimes seem like a difficult and complicated task to figure out what needs to be supplemented and when to supplement. A common question is how to know if the dog is getting enough of everything needed? What supplements should be used and which avoided?

In this section, we will take the guesswork out of making sure your dog has all the minerals needed in the diet. We will look at eleven vital minerals in canine nutrition, discuss why they are needed, in what amounts, and explain how you can make sure your dog is getting enough of them. Though there are quite a few minerals required, most should be present in any healthy diet without the need for supplementation.

Quick Reference

See the quick reference tables below, which provide information on each of the minerals.

Calcium is the most abundant of all minerals found in the body and possibly the most essential. The bones act like the body's calcium "bank"—if there is not enough calcium in the bloodstream for the regulation of the heart muscle, the body withdraws some from the bones. As a result, it can be difficult to tell when your dog is calcium deficient. Dogs can lose up to thirty to forty percent of their bone calcium before any deficiency shows in their blood.

Figure 6.1. Calcium.

Helps with	Found in	Supplement?	Symptoms of Deficiency
Maintaining healthy bones and teeth Activating digestive enzymes and the production of bodily energy Helping blood clot and the transmission of nerve impulses Regulating contractions and the relaxation of muscles and the heart The absorption of vitamin B12	Cheese Yogurt Cottage cheese Canned sardines, mackerel, and salmon Raw meaty bones	Only if feeding a home-cooked diet without bones. If so, use calcium carbonate or calcium citrate.	Problems with the heart and bones

Raw Meaty Bones, or "RMBs," are a great source of calcium, and should be your dog's primary source. Secondary sources should be dairy products like yogurt and cottage cheese (dairy balances itself but doesn't offer enough calcium to balance a whole meal).

If you're feeding your dog a raw diet of forty to fifty percent RMBs and very few grains, you shouldn't need to add any calcium. If your dog is eating a home-cooked diet or is on a raw diet without bones, you'll need to supplement with calcium.

If you need to supplement calcium, calcium carbonate is the best choice, followed by calcium citrate. Both of these are readily absorbed. Bone meal is a poor choice for a calcium supplement because it is also high in phosphorus. Furthermore, computing the proper dose is not as simple as it

With eggshells, simply dry them overnight and then grind them to powder in a coffee grinder. Half a teaspoon of ground eggshell provides approximately 900 milligrams of calcium.

Vitamin D can improve the uptake of calcium. Be careful not to over-supplement calcium—too much can be as dangerous as not enough.

is with straight calcium sources such as calcium citrate and calcium carbonate.

As a rough guide, when feeding a homemade diet that doesn't include RMBs, you should add approximately 900 milligrams of calcium (preferably calcium carbonate) per pound of food served, either in a calcium supplement or by the addition of ground eggshells.

Figure 6.2. Chromium.			
Helps with	Found in	Supplement?	Symptoms of Deficiency
The metabolism of glucose Insulin production	Cheese Muscle meat Liver	No	Problems with the liver's uptake of cholesterol and fatty acids, which can lead to fat buildup in the bloodstream

Figure 6.3. Copper.			
Helps with	Found in	Supplement?	Symptoms of Deficiency
Bone development and elastin The integrity of myelin (nerve covering) Absorbing iron Energy-producing enzymes The oxidation of fatty acids Melanin (a skin pigment) Metabolism of ascorbic acid (vitamin C)	Fish Muscle meat Liver	No	Although deficiencies are rare, symptoms include: Anemia Bone abnormalities

Figure 6.4. Iodine.			
Helps with	Found in	Supplement?	Symptoms of Deficiency
Thyroid gland	Kelp, spirulina, dulce, and irish moss Fish Shellfish	Through additions to the diet, like seaweeds.	Goiters, an unsightly problem in which the thyroid becomes enlarged

Iodine and thyroid issues: Certain foods if fed daily in large amounts can interfere with thyroid production. These include rutabagas, strawberries, peaches, cabbage, peanuts, spinach, and radishes. Limit these foods in your dog's diet if he or she has a thyroid issue. (See the "Sea Vegetables" supplement at the end of this chapter for information on how to add sea vegetables to your dog's diet.)

Figure 6.5. Iron.			
Helps with	Found in	Supplement?	Symptoms of Deficiency
Cell production Fighting anemia	Meat Liver Fish Poultry Fish Eggs	Only if your dog's diet is incomplete.	Listlessness and fatigue Irritability Difficulty swallowing Heart palpitations Pale gums

Of all the minerals, **iron** is the most difficult to provide in sufficient amounts. This is not a big concern for dogs because of the high meat content of most canine diets.

The iron in red meat is the most absorbable and the best form of iron. Supplementation may be needed in the case of some diseases and illnesses; always check with your veterinarian if you suspect your dog may be anemic.

Figure 6.6. Magnesium.			
Helps with	Found in	Supplement?	Symptoms of Deficiency
Bones	Dairy products	Should not be needed if diet is balanced.	Sleep problems
Nerve function	Meat		Depression
Muscle relaxation	Fish		Nervous system conditions such as epilepsy

Figure 6.7. Manganese.			
Helps with	Found in	Supplement?	Symptoms of Deficiency
Enzyme production and metabolism	Seaweeds, including:	Only a small amount is needed, which can be provided through the diet.	Bone deformities
Bone growth and reproduction	Kelp		Cleft palate
Nerve function	Blue-green algae		Poor growth
Muscle relaxation	Spirulina		Reproductive problems
Lowering blood sugar levels			

Figure 6.8. Phosphorus.

Helps with	Found in	Supplement?	Symptoms of Deficiency
Hardness of bones Utilizing fats, proteins and carbohydrates Muscle relaxation Movement of materials in and out of cells Transport of fat in the circulatory system Body's pH buffer system	Dairy products Meat Fish Grains	No. Too much phosphorous is a more common problem than too little.	Too much phosphorus in the diet can lead to bone disease.

After calcium, **phosphorus** is the second most abundant mineral in the body. It is particularly abundant in muscle tissue. Like calcium, phosphorus is also found in the bones.

With phosphorus the problem is more often too much than too little. Because phosphorus binds with calcium, too much phosphorus can deplete your dog's calcium reserves. This can lead to a several serious problems, making the calcium-phosphorous mineral balance very important. Calcium and phosphorus work together and should be balanced in your dog's system at a ratio of 1:1.

If your dog's diet contains a lot of fiber, then up the dog's calcium intake as grains and some plants contain phytates, which make it harder for your dog to absorb calcium.

Since most foods contain good amounts of phosphorus and not much calcium, it is important to understand this balance and add calcium to the diet when needed. This can be done with either raw bones or adding calcium carbonate or calcium citrate.

Figure 6.9. Potassium.

Helps with	Found in	Supplement?	Symptoms of Deficiency
Maintaining cell fluid balance	Dairy products	Only if requested by your vet.	Listlessness
	Meat		Muscle weakness
Glucose conversion	Fish		Spasms
Nerve transmission	Poultry		Rapid heartbeat
Contraction of muscles			
Hormone secretions			

Potassium deficiency is often brought on by the use of steroids or diuretics, which can deplete your dog's reserves. Potassium also works in tandem with sodium, so it is important to keep these two balanced.

Like many minerals, potassium is found in the highest amounts in raw food. Supplementation shouldn't be needed unless specifically requested by your vet.

Figure 6.10. Selenium.

Helps with	Found in	Supplement?	Symptoms of Deficiency
Protecting the heart and liver	Seafood	Deficiency is rare, but if detected, try adding some vitamin E, which aids in the uptake and effectiveness of selenium from dietary sources.	Reproductive problems
Healing skin conditions	Organ meat		Heart problems
	Meat		Weakness in the muscles
Managing some neurological problems like Muscular Dystrophy			
Cancer prevention			

Figure 6.11. Zinc.

Helps with	Found in	Supplement?	Symptoms of Deficiency
Boosts the immune system	Fish Eggs Meat Poultry	Yes	Impaired sense of smell indicated by a lack of appetite Impaired ability to heal Impaired vision Skin problems and hair loss Infertility in males Miscarriage in females

Stress and illness can deplete your dog of **zinc,** as can medications like steroids and diuretics, which interfere with zinc absorption. Unlike some minerals, a zinc deficiency will cause symptoms fairly quickly.

If you do need to supplement with zinc, be careful as this can interfere with the copper levels in the body. These two minerals work together and need to balance each other. If there is too much copper in a dog's system it can hamper zinc absorption. Always check with your veterinarian before deciding to supplement with either one of these minerals.

While you can find zinc in some grains, it is absorbed more readily from meats and eggs. Dogs only require a small amount of zinc in their diets—five to fifteen milligrams does the trick, depending on the dog's weight.

Sea Vegetables

Looking at all these minerals, it can seem like a complex task to meet all of your dog's mineral needs, but with a balanced diet and the right supplementation keeping your dog happy and healthy can be a simple matter.

The best sources of trace minerals are sea vegetables, which are among the richest plant sources of minerals and amino acids. Sea vegetables are an ideal food for dogs, since, unlike most plant sources, they are easy to digest. Seaweeds are rich in protein (about twenty-five percent) and low in salt and fat (around two percent).

Further benefits of nutrient-rich seaweeds include:

- Enhancing the immune system
- Energy Production
- Darkening coat color and skin pigment
- Supporting thyroid function
- Assisting with post-cancer treatment
- Providing extra iodine
- Preventing cancer and fighting tumors
- Preventing heavy metal accumulations
- Assisting the treatment of conditions like diabetes, hypertension, and heart disease

A staple of the Japanese diet for centuries, seaweeds have recently become popular in the United States. Their many benefits for health and longevity are becoming better known. Once considered only a specialty food, you can now find them in most supermarkets.

Now that you know what powerhouses sea vegetables are, which should you use? Like vegetables and vitamins, different sea vegetables can be used at different times and for different reasons. Some of the most common and useful ones are listed in Figure 6.12.

Figure 6.12. Sea Vegetables.

Sea Vegetable	High in	Helps with
Kelp	Vitamins A, B, E, D, and K	Removing heavy metals
Blue-green algae	Iodine	Easing gastric complaints
Spirulina	Protein (60%), chlorophyll (beta-carotene), essential fatty acids, minerals, enzymes, vitamins, and minerals	Thyroid function
Irish Moss		Immune function
Dulce		Stamina
	Protein (60%)	Endurance
	GLA (gamma-linolenic acid)	Inflammation
	Vitamin dense	Fighting cancer
	Calcium, magnesium, and potassium	Blood purification
	Iron	Digestion problems
	Vitamin B-12	Gastritis and ulcers
	Iodine	Bronchitis and lung problems
	Potassium	Strengthens nails and hair
	Trace minerals	Boosts the immune system
		Helps fight viruses
		High in iron, useful for treating anemia

So, How Should I Use Them?

B-Naturals, an online company selling holistic, natural supplements for dogs and cats, has combined high-potency sea vegetables into a product called Berte's Green Blend. This superfood blend takes the guesswork out of supplementation, combining kelp, spirulina, Irish moss, blue-green algae, dulce, alfalfa, and ground fenugreek into a rich blend of minerals, trace minerals, vitamins, and phytonutrients that will go a long way toward keeping your dog healthy. It is designed to promote immunity, endurance, and energy, and is excellent for senior dogs, any dog's coat and skin, and the prevention of arthritis, gastric conditions, allergies, and thyroid problems. If your dog is healthy, a little Berte's Green Blend can help keep him or her that way.

In a Nutshell

Most minerals will be provided through a healthy, varied diet rich in meat, organ meat, fish, and dairy. You should only have to supplement calcium regularly if you're feeding a homemade cooked diet without RMBs.

Remember that supplements like calcium and phosphorous and zinc and copper need to balance each other. Take care when supplementing with these, especially of giving too much. Consult your veterinarian if you're unsure about it.

Sea vegetables are a great source of trace minerals. Added regularly to the diet, they make it easy to ensure that your dog is getting all the necessary trace minerals.

Chapter Seven

Vitamins and Supplements for Canine Health

Giving What They Need

In canine nutrition the word "supplements" can refer to vitamins, herbs, probiotics, digestive enzymes, or amino acids, to name a few. To put it simply, supplements are just things we give our dogs to make sure they are getting enough of everything they need.

Supplements of every kind have enjoyed huge commercial growth in the last decade leading to the now overwhelming range of products on the market. What do our dogs really need? How much? How often?

Supplementing isn't difficult as long as you are careful not to overdo minerals. Because many supplements are sold as combinations, it is easy to overlap your supplementation without realizing it. Look for supplement blends that don't have additional calcium or other minerals. In home-prepared meals we generally add calcium, antioxidants, and omega-3 fatty acids. We may also add probiotics and digestive enzymes if needed. In this chapter we will explain what vitamins dogs need and when, and then show how you can use what you've learned to treat some common canine ailments.

Vitamins

Vitamins are the most popular and recognizable form of supplementation, and probably the most important for your dog. Vitamins come in two categories: water-soluble and fat-soluble.

Water-Soluble Vitamins

Water-soluble vitamins like B and C are easily flushed from the body

Figure 7.1. Water-Soluble Vitamins.

Vitamin	Sources	Helps with	Daily Dosage
Vitamin B	Organ meat Eggs Green leafy vegetables Meat Poultry Fish	Nerve development Kidney function Good muscle tone in the gastrointestinal tract Vision Skin	Dogs up to 25 pounds: 25 milligrams 25- to 50-pound dogs: 25–50 milligrams 50- to 75-pound dogs: 50–100 milligrams 100+-pound dogs: 75–150 milligrams
Vitamin C	Broccoli Brussels sprouts Kale Cabbage Parsley Pineapple Strawberries Spinach Turnip greens Collard greens	Building collagen Adrenal gland functioning Production of lymphocytes Fighting bacteria and viruses Enhancing the effectiveness of chemotherapy drugs Prevention of high blood pressure and serum cholesterol Aiding in the healing of wounds Production of anti-stress hormones	(Minimum): Dogs up to 25 pounds: 100–250 milligrams 25- to 50-pound dogs: 250–500 milligrams 50- to 75-pound dogs: 500–1,000 milligrams 75- to 100-pound dogs: 1,000–2,000 milligrams (Include with each meal)
Bio-flavonoids	Citrus rinds	Antioxidizing Vitamin C absorption Preventing hemorrhages Strengthening capillary walls Preventing bruising Healing inflammatory conditions and arthritis Treatment and prevention of cataracts	For best results, give with vitamin C

so they often need to be given twice daily to be effective. Too much vitamin C can cause diarrhea. If this occurs, back down to a smaller dose.

B VITAMINS

There are eleven B vitamins and they are very important for your dog's health. All the B vitamins tend to work best together, so it is optimal to give them all rather than just one or two.

VITAMIN C WITH BIOFLAVONOIDS

Vitamin C with bioflavonoids is an essential antioxidant and immune-builder for dogs.

While your dog can make some vitamin C, it is often not enough to cope with the daily stresses of life. Dogs need a vitamin C supplement to ease the stress of pollution and illness; additional vitamin C can also help fight allergies. Large doses of C have been shown to help with the immune system and pain relief. Please start vitamin C at the low dose recommendation, and slowly increase the amount each day toward the higher end or therapeutic doses. Should your dog develop diarrhea, back down to the next lowest dose.

The best kind of vitamin C for dogs is calcium ascorbate, which is buffered and easier on the digestive tract than some other kinds.

Bioflavonoids, although not exactly a vitamin, enhance the effectiveness of vitamin C while offering their own benefits. While all the forms of vitamin C are useful, for best results make sure you give your dog C with bioflavonoids.

Fat-Soluble Vitamins

Fat-soluble vitamins like A, D, and E are stored in the dog's fat. They have a longer "life" in the body than water-soluble vitamins and work in tandem with other nutrients.

Figure 7.2. Fat-Soluble Vitamins.

Vitamin	Sources	Helps with	Daily Dosage
Vitamin A	Active: Beef Chicken liver Eggs Dairy Beta-carotene: Fruits Vegetables Carrots Spinach Cantaloupe Kale	Fighting respiratory infections Keeping body tissue healthy Antioxidizing Maintaining good eye function Promoting good reproduction Healthy skin	(Maximum) Dogs up to 25 pounds: 1,000 IU 25- to 50-pound dogs: 2500 IU 50+-pound dogs: 5,000 IU
Vitamin D	Fatty saltwater fish Fish liver oils Fortified dairy products Sunlight	Helps with the metabolism of calcium and phosphorus in the body	(Maximum) Dogs up to 25 pounds: 100 IU 25- to 50-pound dogs: 200 IU 50+-pound dogs: 400 IU
Vitamin E	Whole grains Dark green leafy vegetables Eggs Organ meats	Antioxidizing Fighting cancer Protecting vitamin C and vitamin A from oxidation Aiding circulation Healing of wounds Treating arthritis Regulating the nervous system Athletic performance Prevention of cell damage Aging	Dogs up to 25 pounds: 50–100 IU 25- to 50-pound dogs: 100–200 IU 50- to 75-pound dogs: 200–400 IU 75- to 100-pound dogs: 400–800 IU

VITAMIN A

There are two types of vitamin A. The first type, found in animal sources, is called active vitamin A. The second type, available from plant sources, is beta-carotene. While research has yet to be completed on the use of beta-carotene with dogs, you can be reasonably sure both types of vitamin A will be beneficial for your dog.

Generally food sources are rich enough in this vitamin to satisfy your dog's needs, but there is no harm in adding a little more to increase your dog's immune response, and to help with ulcers, skin problems, and cancer prevention.

VITAMIN D

Vitamin D is the reason we love the sun so much, and why our pets do too. Also considered to be a hormone, it is found in food and sunlight, and can also be supplemented. Too little vitamin D can result in severe health problems, including rickets, stunted growth, delayed tooth development, and bone deformities.

VITAMIN E

Vitamin E works synergistically with omega-3 fatty acids, so make sure vitamin E is given with fish oils.

Digestion Aids

Many dogs on a diet of processed foods miss two vital ingredients: probiotics, the friendly bacteria needed for good digestion, and digestive enzymes, which help break down fats, proteins, and carbohydrates. Heating food over 110 degrees destroys both of these, which means there is very little left in processed dog food by the time it reaches the supermarket. Fresh foods, on the other hand, have these in abundance. Feeding your dog some uncooked food—whether as part of a totally raw diet, or by mixing fresh and dry foods—should give your dog much of the digestive flora and fauna needed for strong, healthy digestion.

PROBIOTICS

Good bacteria include *acidophilus* (*lactobacillus acidophilus*) and *lac-tobacillus bifidus*. These occur naturally in buttermilk, yogurt, aci-dophilus milk, kefir, and some cheeses. Acidophilus can help your dog detoxify, has antibacterial and antifungal properties, and can aid diges-tion and the absorption of nutrients. Berte's Ultra Probiotic Powder, a natural product available from B-Naturals, contains a potent mix-ture of probiotics to keep your dog's digestion running strongly and smoothly.

DIGESTIVE ENZYMES

Dogs need enzymes not only to digest food but for pretty much every function in their bodies such as repairing tissue, nerve cells, bones, and skin.

We add enzymes to a dog's diet when they need assistance with their digestion, particularly with predigesting fats and proteins. (This is often required with dogs suffering liver ailments, pancreatitis, hypothyroidism, diabetes, and gastric illness such as inflammatory bowel disease, irritable bowel syndrome, and colitis.)

> Unripe papayas and pineapples are rich in the enzymes your dog needs to break down proteins, and the bromelain in pineapple can also help with inflammation and the uptake of other supplements.

The three types of enzymes in the body are amylase, protease, and lipase. Amylase helps with the breakdown of carbohydrates, protease with proteins, and lipase with fats. Animal-based enzymes are the most effective aids for fat and protein digestion. Look for the blends pancreatin and pancre-alipase.

Proteolytic enzymes which are the enzymes that help with proteins are also helpful for reducing inflammation, diseases of the respiratory tract, bronchitis, pneumonia, viral diseases, cancer, and arthritis.

Other Supplements

GARLIC

Fresh garlic is dynamite for killing bacteria, fungus, and parasites, as well as providing immune support and normalizing fats in the system. It is also speculated to help repel fleas.

However, do not use garlic for toy breeds of dogs or cats. It is speculated that garlic (and onions) can cause anemia in toy breeds (dogs weighing less than twenty pounds) and cats.

Do start using garlic at a very small amount and gradually increase to the maximum dose. Garlic contains many of the nutrients dogs need including sulfur, potassium, phosphorus, vitamins B and C, allicin, ajoene, amino acids, germanium, and selenium. Remember to always use either fresh garlic or garlic oil as dried garlic is far less effective.

Garlic Maximum Dosage

20- to 25-pound dogs:	⅛ chopped clove
25- to 50-pound dogs:	¼ chopped clove
50- to 75-pound dogs:	¾ chopped clove
100+ pound dogs:	1 chopped clove

ORGANIC APPLE CIDER VINEGAR

Apple cider vinegar (ACV) is high in potassium, as well as many other minerals and trace minerals. Do remember, ACV is alkaline, not acidic.

ACV Minimum Dosage

Dogs up to 25 pounds:	½ teaspoon
25- to 50-pound dogs:	1 teaspoon
50- to 75 pound dogs:	½ tablespoon
75- to 100-pound dogs:	1 tablespoon

Supplements for Specific Health Problems

In "Part III: Remedial Diets Made Simple," we will take a look at specific nutrition and supplement advice for different conditions in more detail. To put what we have learned about supplements to use, here are the most common canine ailments and the best supplements to treat them. With this guide you'll be able to get a much better sense of what your dog needs to remedy his or her specific health problems and you will get the extra satisfaction of taking much more responsibility for the health and well-being of your dog.

Always remember to consult with your veterinarian for the treatment and diagnosis of any illness. These suggestions are not meant as a substitute for proper medical treatment. For more detailed information see "Part II: Feeding Your Dog the Easy Way" and "Part III: Remedial Diets Made Simple."

Figure 7.3. Vitamins and Supplements.	
Condition	Treat with
Allergies	Digestive enzymes
	Vitamin C with bioflavonoids
	Bromelain
	EPA fish oil
	DMG (N-Dimethyglycine)
Arthritis and Joint Problems	EPA fish oil
	Glucosamine and Chondroitin blends (Flexile Plus)
	Berte's Green Blend
	Vitamin C with bioflavonoids
	Berte's Ultra Probiotic Powder
	Bromelain
	Yucca
	Willow Bark
	Vitamin E

Figure 7.3. Vitamins and Supplements. (continued)

Condition	Treat with
Bladder/Kidney Infections (For more information see "Chapter Twenty-One: Diet and Kidney Needs.")	Berte's Probiotic Powder B complex COQ10 (CoEnzyme Q10) Cranberry juice capsules
Cancer (For more information see "Chapter Twenty: Diets for Dogs with Cancer.")	Antioxidants EPA fish oil Mushroom extracts (liquid tinctures) Bertes Immune Blend (antioxidants, enzymes, probiotics, l-glutamine, l-arginine, vitamins A and D) CoEnzyme Q10
Cardiovascular Problems (For more information see "Chapter Nineteen: Heart-Healthy Diets.")	EPA fish oil L-carnitine (amino acid) L-taurine (amino acid)
Colitis, Irritable Bowel Disease, and Gastritis (For more information see "Chapter Twenty-Eight: Diet and Gastric Problems.")	Berte's Ultra Probiotic Powder L-glutamine Digestive enzymes such as pancreatin and pancrealipase
Dermatitis (Flaking skin, itching, and hair loss)	EPA fish Oil Berte's Ultra Probiotic Powder Nettle tinctures Vitamin E Vitamin C with bioflavonoids
Diarrhea (For more information see "Chapter Twenty-Two: Diet and Gastric Problems.")	Canned or fresh pulped pumpkin Berte's Ultra Probiotic Powder

Figure 7.3. Vitamins and Supplements. (continued)	
Condition	Treat with
Ear Infections (Yeast)	L-taurine (also found in meat) Magnesium B complex
Epilepsy	DMG (N-Dimethyglycine)
Hypothyroid	Green foods such as kelp, dulce, and spirulina
Kennel Cough	Vitamin C with bioflavonoids (given often throughout the day) Echinacea and goldenseal tincture (given three times a day)
Motion Sickness	Ginger Vitamin C with bioflavonoids
Pancreatitis (See "Chapter Twenty-Three: Diet and Pancreatitis.")	Pancreatin Digestive enzymes Berte's Ultra Probiotic Powder Berte's Digestion Blend EPA fish oil*

---

* All fish oil doses are 1,000 mg per ten pounds of body weight daily

Part II

Feeding Your Dog
the Easy Way

Chapter Eight

Feeding Homemade Diets the Easy Way

As Easy as 1-2-3

We've been told so many times over the years that the only "complete and balanced" diets for dogs are those on supermarket shelves that many of us have come to believe it. Fresh-food diets, the story goes, are dangerous and unhealthy—dogs can't eat table food! But some of us are old enough to remember a time prior to mass-marketed processed pet foods, a time when pets would eat raw and cooked foods, table scraps, or whatever they could find in the wild and do just fine.

A move toward a homemade diet is a move back toward a more natural one. And while it takes some real courage to get past all the brainwashing and start taking responsibility for your pet's health and nutrition, you'll be amazed how simple it is once you start.

The most important thing you'll be doing for your dog is changing his or her diet to one consisting primarily of fresh food, whether raw or cooked. The difference between fresh and processed foods, as we humans are now finding, is like night and day. The only advantage offered by commercial pet foods is convenience. It's no different than stopping at a fast food restaurant to pick up a meal for yourself, or popping a "heat and serve" dinner from the grocery store into the microwave—you don't kid yourself that it's better for you, you do it because it's easy. But there's no convenience in having to take care of a sick, unhappy pet whose body is giving way from eating junk food all his or her life. If you want your pet to live a long, happy life, you need to start to look at canine nutrition differently, even if it takes a little time, experimentation, and effort.

Following the easy steps laid out in these chapters, you should start to see results in no time at all. Within a couple of weeks your dog, no matter how old he or she is, will be sporting a healthier coat and skin, have more energy, better breath—the list goes on. You'll be amazed at the transformation.

This part of the book takes the guesswork and hassle out of preparing your pets' meals. First we'll take a look at the supplies you'll need to make the switch, and then we'll move on to some basic home feeding rules. In upcoming chapters we'll get into the nuts and bolts of feeding raw and cooked diets, covering everything you need to know to start feeding your dog a healthy, tasty, home-cooked diet he or she will love.

Getting Started: What You'll Need

There are a few basic things you'll need to make feeding your new homemade diet truly easy. You probably already have many of these items at home.

FREEZER

A freezer is essential for most home feeders. Having a big freezer allows you to purchase and store foods in bulk, making the whole process more economical and allowing you to get past that old myth that feeding a homemade diet is more expensive than a commercial processed one. The bigger the freezer the better!

SCISSORS

A good pair of meat scissors is invaluable for cutting meats like chicken and ribs into pieces that are manageable for your dog's size.

PLASTIC BINS, CONTAINERS, AND ZIP-LOCK BAGS

These are essential for storing meat in the freezer and for thawing it out in the fridge.

MIXING BOWLS

You will need a few of these for putting everything together. The bigger your dog, the bigger the bowls you need.

KNIVES

A good sharp set of knives is essential for preparing raw meals, and comes in handy for cooked meals too. They'll need to be sharpened regularly, especially if you've got a small dog since their meals usually require more cutting and preparation.

REFRIGERATOR SPACE

The easiest way to feed raw, as we'll soon see, is to buy meats in bulk and store them in the freezer. To do this you'll need some fridge space set aside to thaw each meal and to store leftovers.

FOOD SCALE

A small food scale is useful for measuring food, at least until you become used to what constitutes proper serving sizes.

MEAT GRINDER

A grinder is particularly useful for people with small and toy dogs and for those who are uncomfortable feeding whole bones. If you're going to feed raw, a meat grinder is a great investment.

Ingredients for Homemade Diets

So, you're asking, now that I have the equipment, which foods do I need and how can I get them? First, let's take a look at the types of food you'll need, starting with the staples of your new homemade diet: muscle and organ meats.

MUSCLE MEAT

Muscle meat is just flesh that doesn't include any bone. An excellent source of animal proteins, it should form a good part of your dog's new diet.

Figure 8.1. Muscle Meat.	
Beef heart	Lamb heart
Ground turkey	Ground lamb
Rabbit	Chicken hearts and gizzards
Fish (fillet)	Turkey hearts
Tongue	Wild game (buffalo, venison, elk, llama, goat, ostrich, or kangaroo)
Ground chicken	
Ground beef	

ORGAN MEAT

Organ meats are full of nutrients and vitamins and should make up five to ten percent of any homemade diet. They are rich, though, so they shouldn't exceed this amount.

Figure 8.2. Organ Meats.	
Beef liver and kidney	Chicken liver
Lamb liver and kidney	Turkey liver
Pork liver	

Are the Basic Ingredients the Same for Raw and Cooked Diets?

Mostly, with some slight variations here and there. Muscle and organ meats should be included in any homemade diet, raw or cooked. Raw diets, as we'll learn about in the next chapter, also include Raw Meaty Bones (RMBs). Because it's dangerous to feed cooked bones, bones don't form part of a cooked diet unless you're prepared to offer them raw. You can also offer some eggs and dairy (try plain yogurt and cottage cheese) as part of a cooked or raw diet. We'll look at other ingredients like vegetables and grains in the raw and cooked feeding chapters.

Ok, So Where Do I Get All this Stuff?

Good question! There are a number of ways to get the food you'll need for your new diet. Most grocery stores should have many of these foods on hand. I work with my local supermarket meat manager to order beef heart and kidney, chicken hearts, and pork neck bones. All grocery stores should carry chicken wings and leg quarters, and some meat departments will also be able to order chicken necks and backs for you. The meats you have access to will obviously vary by location. In my area, I'm able to get chicken, lamb, beef, and pork. If the local grocery store near you doesn't carry the items you need and won't order them for you, check local ethnic grocery stores or butcher shops.

If you're having trouble sourcing some of the above food from the supermarket or butcher, look for a local raw feeding list or group. These groups are a good way of connecting with people in your area who know the ropes of sourcing food for homemade diets. Some locales even have raw meat co-op groups that place group orders, making it cheaper for everyone.

> A list of sources by state that sell frozen and fresh meat is available at dogaware.com.

For dog owners used to buying commercial food, this new way of shopping and feeding can seem overwhelming at first, but once you've got yourself set up and have found where to get your meat, it is easy to get used to.

Commandments of Home Feeding

To make sure your new homemade diet is truly "complete and balanced," there are a few basic rules you need to follow. Within a couple of months they'll become second nature.

Feed According to Weight

Start by feeding around two to three percent of the dog's body weight in food daily, divided into two meals. Larger dogs may need less than this and smaller dogs may need more, as smaller dogs have faster metabolisms. Dogs are as individual as we are, so the table below is just a guide. You may need to make adjustments in the amount of food you feed depending on how the diet affects the dog's weight. Two to three percent is just a starting point.

Figure 8.3. Amount of Food Needed.	
100-pound dog:	2–3 pounds daily, or two meals of 1–1.5 pounds each
75-pound dog:	1.5–2 pounds daily, or two meals of 12–18 ounces each
50-pound dog:	1–1.5 pounds daily, or two meals of 8–12 ounces each
25-pound dog:	8–12 ounces daily, or two meals of 4–6 ounces each

Don't Overfeed

Though dogs are always trying to convince you to do otherwise, don't overfeed them. Overfeeding is one of the main causes of diarrhea, digestive upset, and obesity.

Variety Comes over Time, Not with One Meal

Many owners try to find one meal that contains what they consider to be an ideal mix of nutrients and proceed to feed that every night without variation. Can you imagine how bored you would be if you were fed the same dinner every night, not to mention the health problems you might develop from only one set of nutrients? Your dog needs variety, for both his or her taste buds and well-being.

Dogs have the ability to "train" their owners into feeding them only a few foods by refusing new things that are offered, leading to a diet that can seriously compromise their health. Vets often use this potential pitfall as a reason to avoid home-prepared diets. The trick is to always vary the diet. A diet consisting of a good variety of foods provides the wide range of nutrients your dog needs, which can't be accomplished in one meal. If it turns out your dog likes one of your new home-cooked meals and not the others you offer, keep trying different combinations of food until he or she is getting the necessary variety.

Be Patient!

Making the switch will mean a number of adjustments for you and your dog. If you find it to be a lot of work, or your dog isn't responding to the new food as you'd hoped, just be patient. It can take a while sometimes, especially if you're switching from a way of feeding that you've both been used to for years. Keep in mind what a positive change this new way of feeding will bring about and remain happy and enthusiastic at mealtimes. Keep trying out different meals and different combinations and it shouldn't be long until you have a salivating, energetic, happy home-fed dog.

Smaller dogs, especially toy breeds, sometimes need to eat more than two to three percent of their body weight, and often do better with three smaller meals each day.

Puppies under the age of six months require more frequent meals (three to four per day) and need a bit more calcium (1,500 milligrams per pound of food served) to help them grow. Puppies will eat about ten percent of their body weight at eight weeks of age, or two to three percent of their anticipated adult weight. (For more information, see "Chapter Twelve: Feeding Your Puppy.")

Chapter Nine

Feeding Raw the Easy Way

The Easiest Way to Feed

If you've ever made a salad, you know making raw food is easy—it's just a matter of finding the right ingredients, cutting them up, and putting them all together. It's the same with feeding your dog raw foods. Still, if this new way of feeding seems foreign or even a little overwhelming at first—especially after years of feeding commercial dog foods—don't worry. You'll get the hang of it in no time and your dog will love you for it. This chapter shows how easy it is to prepare homemade raw meals, and to offer your dog the kind of nutrition that really serves his or her health and longevity.

Though our anatomies are different, there is one essential principle of human nutrition that also holds true for our dogs: fresh, raw food is best. Let's start looking after our dogs like we do the rest of our family. The most difficult part will be grasping the concept and getting used to new ways of feeding. The easiest part will be watching your dog's enthusiasm when he or she gets into the raw diet!

Ingredients for a Raw Diet

Now let's take a look at what you'll need to feed your dog a varied and delicious raw diet. A healthy raw diet should include a good variety of the muscle and organ meats we learned about in the previous chapter, but with one very important addition: Raw Meaty Bones (RMBs).

Shiloh's Story

Shiloh, a female golden retriever puppy, is a great example of the rejuvenating effect of raw food. Struck down by a severe case of demodectic mange while still very young, Shiloh was surrendered into rescue at just eight months of age with no hair on her face, chest, stomach, and legs. Her skin was so dry and cracked that just touching her would cause her to bleed. Her face was so badly affected she could hardly open her eyes, and she was understandably depressed by her condition.

Joanie, who was running the rescue program at the time Shiloh was brought in, agreed to foster her, and quickly set about trying to cure her debilitating condition through diet. After switching her over to raw food, Joanie began supplementing Shiloh's diet with Berte's Immune Blend, Berte's Ultra Probiotic Powder, and fish oil.

The change was dramatic. Within a week Shiloh started to show real improvement. Hair started to grow all over her body, and before long the light came on in her eyes. Soon she was happily swimming, retrieving, and playing with her two big foster brothers.

Joanie is proud to say that today Shiloh is healthy, smart, and, most importantly, happy—a living testament to the restorative powers of a healthy, homemade diet. As for Joanie and her family, they can't imagine life without Shiloh, their "ugly duckling" turned "Cinderella!"

Raw Meaty Bones

RMBs are rich in things your dog loves and needs—including meat, bone, and fat—and are an excellent source of calcium. Some good choices of RMBs include:

- Chicken, all parts including wings, backs, necks, and leg quarters

- Duck necks
- Turkey necks, cut up
- Pork necks, breast, tails, and feet
- Beef ribs, necks, and tails
- Lamb ribs, necks, and breast
- Rabbit, all parts including front and hindquarters and back
- Canned fish with bones, such as mackerel, pink salmon, and sardines

Worried about Feeding Bones?

If you are apprehensive about feeding whole bones to your dog, you can buy the bones ground or get a grinder and grind them yourself. Only do what you feel comfortable doing.

The large bones of bigger animals like pigs, cows, and sheep (legs, femurs, and sometimes beef rib and neck bones) can be too much of a mouthful for dogs, but even these can still be given as recreational bones (though they shouldn't be considered part of the dietary balance).

Getting Ready to Feed Raw

Now that you have your supplies and food, you are ready to get started. You may be wondering if you should transition to a raw diet slowly or make the change all at once. There's no black-and-white answer. At my house all I have is raw food so any dog that comes my way starts on a varied raw diet right away. I take in and feed rescues and so far I haven't had any problems. So this seems to be a good sign!

The transition is an individual matter, and you should change your dog's diet at a rate at which you feel comfortable. If you have all the foods and supplies and feel ready to start feeding raw immediately—following, of course, the instructions on how to offer a varied and complete diet—then do it. If you want to start introducing raw food slowly, until both you and your pet are used to the new diet, then that's fine too. Some people choose to convert to a raw diet more slowly by adding muscle meat to the commercial food first; others alternate between raw meal and kibble meals for a time, gradually phasing out the processed food. The important thing is that you feel comfortable, and that you are moving toward feeding your dog a complete fresh-food diet. (To learn more about combining fresh food with commercial foods, see "Chapter Eleven: No Quibble with Kibble.")

Can My Dog Get Sick from the Bacteria in Raw Food?

Renowned vet and author Dr. Richard Pitcairn, who has been working with dogs all his life, reports that in fifteen years of recommending raw meat he has never seen a case of *E. Coli* or *salmonella* in his patients. The key is to take the same care and safety in handling meat for a dog as you would for yourself. Only buy fresh meat and freeze portions that they're not going to eat straight away.

But My Dog's Too Picky!

Some dogs may have preferences for some meats over others, so there will be a good deal of trial and error at first and a few times when your dog might turn his or her nose up. Don't get discouraged when you first start out—some dogs need time to get used to the texture, temperature, and flavor of meat, whereas other dogs will act like they've been waiting for raw food their whole lives. Some dogs do better if they're fed in their crates individually and away from other dogs. It's up to you to see how your dog responds and to go from there. (For more information, see "Chapter Eighteen: Picky Eaters.")

Feeding Time!

The best way to plan each day's meal is to head to the freezer the night before and put everything you're planning on feeding the next day in plastic containers to thaw overnight. Always make sure the meat is fully thawed before serving.

Mixing It Up

I usually feed muscle meat for the first meal of the day and RMBs for the second, but this is my preference and you're welcome to switch it around. Likewise, some experimentation can be done with the number of meals. Some people prefer to feed just once a day. While this is OK, be sure to alternate the meals by feeding RMBs one day and muscle and organ meat the next, or half RMBs and half muscle meat at each meal. What's important is to remember to balance the diet over time, rather than at each meal.

Don't rely on just one type of RMB, like chicken. Rotate between poultry, pork, beef, and other meats for variety. I feed chicken necks and backs for three nights, pork necks and tails for two nights, and beef or lamb ribs for the last two nights to ensure a good variety of bones each week.

For meat meals I feed tripe twice a week, beef heart once or twice, chicken hearts once, and ground lamb or beef for the other meals. Some days I may add eggs or dairy (plain yogurt or cottage cheese), and I add some kidney or liver to some of the meals to make sure that their five to ten percent quota of organ meat is met. Again, try not to rely on one type of muscle meat, like ground beef. Variety over time is crucial for a balanced raw diet.

Some people swear by adding ground or pulverized vegetables, which can offer dogs some good nutrients. I would keep any vegetable mix to less than one-quarter of the diet, as vegetables add bulk to the stool and can cause gas.

In time you'll develop a system of feeding that works best for you and your lifestyle. Additionally, asking someone experienced with raw feeding or joining an email group with members who are familiar with this kind of diet helps a lot when you have questions or concerns.

What about the Mineral Balance?

Along with the basic rules we learned in the last chapter, there is one more thing that is important to remember when feeding raw: the calcium to phosphorus ratio. The best way to maintain a healthy balance is to feed two meals per day, the first being an RMB meal, and the second made up of muscle and organ meats. Eggs, dairy, and vegetables can also be added to the second meal. A diet consisting of forty to fifty percent RMBs provides all the calcium a dog needs.

Sample Raw Diets

To give you an extra helping hand with getting started, the following list gives you four days' worth of balanced diets that will give your dog a great variety of tastes, textures, and nutrients. Quantities are for a fifty-pound dog.

SAMPLE DIET ONE

Morning

6 ounces (¾ cup) beef heart

2 ounces (¼ cup) beef kidney

1 egg

Evening

8–12 ounces (1–1½ cups) chicken necks or backs

SAMPLE DIET TWO

Morning

6 ounces (¾ cup) ground beef

2 ounces (¼ cup) cottage cheese

2 ounces (¼ cup) ground broccoli

Evening

8–12 ounces (1–1½ cups) pork ribs

SAMPLE DIET THREE

Morning

> 6 ounces (¾ cup) pork chunks or ground pork
>
> 2 ounces (¼ cup) pork liver
>
> 2 ounces (1/4 cup) plain yogurt

Evening

> 8–12 ounces (1–1½ cups) turkey necks (cut into 3–4 sections)

SAMPLE DIET FOUR

Morning

> 6 ounces (¾ cup) green tripe (unbleached)
>
> 4 ounces (½ cup) beef kidney

Evening

> 8–12 ounces (1–1½ cups) chicken wings

So, Are You Ready?

While preparing a raw diet takes some getting used to in the beginning, any effort you make will seem like nothing when you see how happy and energetic your dog is after eating raw for a few weeks.

Not only does the raw diet offer your dog the best bio-available protein and nutrients, it gives you complete control over the quality of your dog's diet, which is really satisfying. In a broader sense, once you learn your way around vitamins and supplements and how to treat different health conditions, you can start taking more responsibility for your pet's overall health, varying the diet according to what you think he or she needs. You and your dog will soon be wondering what took you so long!

Supplements for Raw Feeding

We've already examined what supplements to use when your dog gets sick. Here are three great supplements you can add to the raw diet daily to keep your dog in great shape:

- Berte's Immune Blend (for healthy dogs, use half the regular dose)
- Berte's Green Blend
- EPA fish oil or salmon oil capsules (one 1,000-milligram capsule daily per twenty pounds of body weight)

Further Reading

There are two books I recommend having by your side if you're starting to feed raw: *Switching to Raw,* by Susan Johnson (www.switchingtoraw.com) and *Raw Meaty Bones,* by Dr. Tom Lonsdale (www.rawmeatybones.com). Both are invaluable in helping with the transition and learning more about your dog's nutritional needs.

Another great resource for raw feeders is Mary Straus's collection of raw feeding sources, websites, and books at www.dogaware.com.

If you're looking to invest in a meat grinder, the Maverick grinder works quite well and can be picked up at Pierce Equipment (www.pierceequipment.com/grinders.html).

Chapter Ten

Feeding Cooked Diets the Easy Way

Cooking at Home

If you don't like the idea of feeding raw—and many people don't—then a home-cooked diet using fresh ingredients is the next best thing. And it doesn't have to be one way or the other—you can experiment with the diet according to your comfort level. If you want to feed mainly cooked food but with RMBs, or a mixture of raw and cooked food, then great. There are no hard and fast rules for what to feed, other than to make sure the diet you choose is balanced and complete.

The Five Cooked-Food Commandments

Along with the fundamental home-feeding rules we've learned about already, there are a few important things to remember about feeding cooked food.

1. ADD CALCIUM

If you're feeding a diet without bones, always balance the home-cooked meal with either calcium carbonate (900 milligrams per pound of food served) or half a teaspoon of ground eggshell.

2. VARIETY IS KEY

Feeding cooked food allows you a great degree of variety. Along with the normal meats you can bake fresh fish or use canned varieties like mackerel, salmon, and sardines. These canned fish contain steamed bones that are safe for your dog and provide all the calcium he or she needs for that meal.

3. FIFTY TO SEVENTY-FIVE PERCENT ANIMAL PROTEIN

Animal protein sources like meat, organs, eggs, and dairy should make up at least fifty percent of the diet (seventy-five percent is ideal). Keep in mind that a diet of seventy-five percent meat, yogurt, eggs, etc., is not a diet that is seventy-five percent protein. These foods also contain water, fat, and some fiber.

4. VEGETABLES FOR THE REST

Use vegetables for the rest of the diet. In order to make them suitable for your dog's digestive system, they must be fully boiled or steamed and then mashed or pureed in a food processor. Once they're mashed or pureed you can freeze them to use later along with your meats. Variety also applies to vegetable choices—the more you vary what you offer, the more interested your dog will be and the more nutrients he or she will get.

5. KEEP GRAINS TO A MINIMUM

If you want to use grains make sure they make up less than one-sixth of the diet. Grains increase the size of the stool and some dogs can't digest them at all. Start slowly and wait to see how your dog reacts to them and go from there.

Getting Ready to Feed Cooked

Now that we know the basic rules, let's take a look at how to put together some simple recipes. The basic formula I like to follow is seventy-five percent animal protein and fat sources with twenty-five percent vegetable matter. The diet you feed will vary according to your dog's tastes, condition, and needs, but a three-to-one ratio is a good rule of thumb for home-cooked feeding. Dogs need as much good-quality protein as you can give them, so always err on the side of too much rather than too little.

As with raw meals, the easiest way to prepare cooked meals is to make large batches in advance and freeze them, thawing them the night before you need them. If you do it this way remember to add the supplements right before serving as freezing can compromise their integrity. Always keep canned fish, canned tripe, and dairy on hand to feed in case you forget to prepare meals in advance. These also come in handy for road trips, if you're boarding your dog, or if you leave your dog in the care of a pet sitter.

Deb's Story

Deb has three Bichons who are eight, nine, and twelve years old. Because all three are rescues, she doesn't know much about their lives before she took them into her care. What she does know is that they were very sick. "They have all had various health problems," she says. "Chronic ear infections, irritable bowel syndrome, chronic hot spots, constant itchy skin, yeasty feet from constant licking, tear staining, lethargy, coarse hair, hair loss, impacted anal glands, and arthritis." With vets unable to provide any effective treatment, she tried every kibble on the market in the hope of some improvement. "Nothing helped," she says. "I was at my wit's end."

After finding my website and researching home-prepared diets, Deb began feeding a home-cooked diet free of grains and chemicals, which she realized were the root causes of all her dogs' ailments. The change, she says, couldn't have been more positive. "I can now honestly say that all of my dogs' problems are gone. They are living happy, healthy lives and love mealtimes."

Ingredients for Cooked-Food Diets

If you want to feed a cooked diet, any of the meats we looked at in "Chapter Eight: Feeding Homemade Diets the Easy Way" are suitable for cooking (excluding the RMBs, of course). To make the choice even easier, there's a list in Figure 10.1 of meats I recommend especially for home cooking, along with some other foods that can help you meet your dog's animal protein needs.

Figure 10.1. Recommended Foods for Home-Cooked Diets.	
Muscle meat	**Organ meat**
Beef	Beef liver and kidney
Chicken	Chicken liver and kidney
Lamb	Lamb liver and kidney
Pork	Pork liver and kidney
Turkey	
Mackerel, salmon, or sardines (canned)	
Heart (meat can be ground or in pieces)	
Dairy	**Other**
Yogurt	Eggs
Cottage cheese	Tripe (canned)
	Healthy leftovers

For the vegetable portion of the meal, offer a variety of the vegetables listed in Figure 10.2.

Figure 10.2. Vegetables.	
Broccoli	Sweet potato
Cabbage	Carrots
Zucchini	Yellow summer squash
Cauliflower	Kale
Spinach	Mustard greens

For dogs with arthritis or joint problems, it's best to avoid the nightshade vegetables (white potatoes, tomatoes, eggplant, and peppers), as these can exacerbate irritation.

Sample Cooked-Food Diets

SAMPLE DIET ONE

> 12 ounces (1½ cups) beef
> 4 ounces (½ cup) plain yogurt
> 2 ounces (¼ cup) liver
> 6 ounces (¾ cup) pureed sweet potato
> 1,350 milligrams calcium
> 2 EPA 1,000-milligram fish oil capsules
> 1½ teaspoons Berte's Immune Blend

SAMPLE DIET TWO

> 12 ounces (1½ cup) chicken
> 2 ounces (¼ cup) cottage cheese
> 1 egg
> 2 ounces (¼ cup) beef kidney
> 6 ounces (¾ cup) (combined) cooked cabbage and zucchini
> 1,350 milligrams calcium
> 2 EPA 1,000-milligram fish oil capsules
> 1½ teaspoons Berte's Immune Blend

Sample Cooked Recipes

This recipe makes two meals for a fifty-pound dog. For a hundred-pound dog, double the amounts. For a twenty-five pound dog, cut the recipe in half. In all cases, divide the recipe into two meals.

Remember to add 900 milligrams of calcium per pound of food served.

Instead of ground beef or chicken, you can use canned salmon, mackerel, turkey, lamb, beef heart, or ground pork.

Vegetables can be mixed and matched; use any from the list earlier in this chapter. If you are out of dairy products or eggs, add more meat.

Supplements for a Cooked Diet

A cooked diet requires different daily supplements than a raw diet. Make sure you offer your dog the following with his or her cooked meal:

- Calcium (900 milligrams per pound of food served).
- EPA fish oil capsules (one capsule, containing 180 milligrams EPA/120 milligrams DHA, daily per twenty to thirty pounds of body weight).
- Vitamin E (50 IU daily per ten pounds of body weight)
- Vitamin C (100 to 200 IU daily per ten pounds of body weight)
- Vitamin B complex (25 milligrams daily for dogs up to fifty pounds; 50 milligrams daily for dogs over fifty pounds)

Aside from calcium, you shouldn't need to add minerals to the diet; the variety of foods you offer should provide everything your dog needs.

If you're in the process of changing your dog's diet, probiotics and digestive enzymes can be helpful. Try Berte's Immune Blend, which contains vitamin C, vitamin E, B complex, enzymes, and probiotics. For a daily vitamin blend without enzymes and probiotics, there is also Berte's Daily Blend, which is a great source of trace minerals.

Chapter Eleven

No Quibble with Kibble

Mixing It Up

If you're still deciding whether you want to change the way you feed your dogs, don't worry. There are lots of people out there who, for a variety of reasons, aren't willing to switch completely to a raw or home-cooked diet. They might be uncomfortable with this new way of feeding, or feel they don't have the time, money, or the expertise to do it every day.

The chapter that follows will help alleviate some of the anxieties people feel about changing their dogs' diets. Changing the diet doesn't have to be an all or nothing affair—far from it. You can do only what you feel comfortable with. So with that in mind, let's take a look at simple ways you can improve your dog's nutrition by supplementing his or her current processed diet with fresh foods.

Making Up for Lost Nutrients

Whatever the labels say and no matter how happy the dogs look on the ads, commercial foods are made up of processed, sterilized, and denatured foods, foods that simply can't offer the optimum nutrition fresh foods contain. And while commercial diets may offer all the nutrients suggested by the pet food industry, they are still no substitute for fresh food. How can they make up for all the fragile nutrients lost in cooking and processing, nutrients like omega-3 fatty acids, vitamins B and C, and essential amino acids?

The answer is, they can't. Fresh foods provide a variety of nutrients and flavors that processed foods don't, making it easier for you to offer your pet a complete diet.

The palatability and freshness of fresh foods can really come in handy when your dog, for whatever reason—be it illness, travel, or stress—has a loss of appetite. It's also really satisfying for you to provide the nutrition that may have been missing from his or her diet, and to see how much happier he or she is as a result!

Giving Your Dog What He or She Needs

If you're adding foods to a diet high in commercial, processed foods, lay off the carbohydrates since your dog will already be getting more than his or her fair share! Instead, focus on adding fresh animal protein and fats

Figure 11.1. Recommended Foods to Add to Commercial Diets.	
Ground beef	Goat
Beef heart and liver	Mackerel, sardines, or salmon (canned)
Pork	Eggs
Lamb	Whole-milk yogurt
Chicken	Cottage cheese
Turkey	

The sample cooked and raw diets we've seen already in this section of the book can be used alongside commercial food—just vary the amounts according to how much (or how little) fresh food you want to add to the diet, and be careful not to overfeed.

What about Calcium?

If you're adding more than fifty percent fresh food (not including RMBs) to kibble, you'll need to add some calcium in the form of eggshells or a supplement. If

Organ meats, like kidney and liver, can be added in small amounts twice a week.

you're just using fresh food for a few days to get a finicky eater to eat, or as a temporary appetite stimulus for a dog recuperating from an illness, the calcium balance is not as important. If you continue to supplement with fresh foods over time, be sure to add calcium (900 milligrams per pound of food) to foods that don't contain it already (anything aside from RMBs, commercial pet foods, and canned fish with soft steamed bones).

Sample Mixed Diets

To help you get started, let's look at some sample diets. While the recipes offer about an equal ratio of kibble to fresh food, you can vary that to one-to-three or three-to-one, and so on. I've included digestive enzymes and probiotic powder to help ease digestion during the transition. While many dogs may not need these, it's good to use them for a while at the beginning, at least until you and your dog are comfortable with this new diet. Feel free to mix these recipes according to what your dog likes, which foods are available, and what you feel comfortable feeding, using any combination of the foods listed earlier this chapter.

Sample Kibble and Fresh-Food Diet

Quantity is for a fifty-pound dog.

Morning Meal

- 1 teaspoon Berte's Daily Blend
- 2 1,000-milligram capsules EPA fish oil
- 1 tablet Berte's Zymes
- ¼ teaspoon ground eggshell
- 2 ounces (¼ cup) premium kibble
- 2 ounces (¼ cup) meat (ground beef, beef heart, ground chicken, turkey, or lamb)
- 1 egg

2 tablespoons whole-milk yogurt

½ teaspoon Berte's Ultra Probiotic Powder

Evening Meal

Small amount of liver every other day

2 tablespoons cottage cheese

1 teaspoon Berte's Daily Blend

½ teaspoon Berte's Ultra Probiotic Powder

2 1,000-milligram capsules EPA fish oil

¼ teaspoon ground eggshell

2 ounces (¼ cup) premium kibble

4 ounces (½ cup) canned water-packed mackerel, salmon, or
sardines; beef kidney; chicken hearts; ground pork; or tripe
(use a variety of these items)

1 tablet Berte's Zymes

Switching to Homemade

So you've supplemented the processed diet with fresh food for a while,
and now you're interested in transitioning your dog from commercial
pet food to a more natural homemade diet. But you don't want to do
it all at once. So how do you do it?

First, keep adding fresh foods to the kibble, and then slowly reduce
the amount of dry dog food over time. Keep up with the digestive supplements (Berte's Ultra Probiotic Powder or Berte's Zymes) if you're
worried about how your dog will cope with all the new food. In most
cases these products will only be needed for the first two or three
months of the new diet, but keep an eye on your dog—if he or she
seems to still be struggling with digestion, keep up with the powder
and enzymes.

Sometimes it just takes a bit of confidence to make the switch.
Before long, the change authenticates itself. When you see how much
your dog enjoys the fresh food, not to mention the physical improvements in his or her coat, teeth, and attitude, you'll have all the motivation you need!

Chapter Twelve

Feeding Your Puppy

Using What You Already Know

Feeding your puppy can seem like a tricky business sometimes, but it doesn't have to be. You just need to add a few simple rules and recipes to what you already know. With a bit of reorientation you'll be well on your way to a healthy feeding routine.

There's absolutely nothing to be afraid of when feeding your puppy a homemade diet. In fact, there's everything to be excited about; feeding your puppy at home gives you the chance to offer her much better nutrition than she'd get on a commercial diet. And it's satisfying to be able to take responsibility for her health and diet from the very beginning, whether he or she is twelve hours old or you've just brought him or her home after a few months. Plus, if you start feeding at home when at an early age, by the time your dog is an adult you'll be a pro.

Most of the rules of feeding adults hold true for puppies. Protein is essential for healthy coat, skin, bones, and organs, and you should always err on the side of more rather than less. Calcium, so essential for growing bones, should be given in the form of RMBs or added via supplements to a home-cooked RMB-free diet (remember not to add calcium if you're feeding a commercial diet.)

But there are some important differences we'll look at in this chapter, particularly with very young puppies. So let's go back to the beginning and take a look at the first thing you'll need to know: how to wean and raise your dog on a homemade diet.

Weaning and Raising Puppies on a Raw Diet

WEEKS ONE THROUGH FOUR

There's no better food in the world to feed puppies less than four weeks old than their mother's milk. Perfectly designed for a puppy's digestive system, it's the very definition of a "complete and balanced" whole food, containing all the nutrients a puppy needs in the right amounts. While you might be tempted to add to your puppy's diet during the first few weeks, be careful—until a puppy is four weeks old, his or her digestive system is not equipped to digest any other whole food. Occasionally, you might find yourself having to supplement a puppy's diet due to insufficient milk production, a large litter, or the absence, sickness, or death of the puppy's mother. Although it's impossible to reproduce mother's milk exactly, when supplementation is necessary, use a substitute that is as close to mother's milk as possible.

Mother's Milk Replacement Formula for Puppies up to Four Weeks of Age

1 pint of goat's milk, either fresh in cartons from the store or evaporated (if using evaporated, be sure to dilute with water as directed).

2 egg yolks

2 1,000-milligram capsules EPA fish oil capsules

½ teaspoon Berte's Ultra Probiotic Powder

4 to 6 tablespoons whole-milk yogurt

The egg yolks give your puppy the extra protein he or she needs for growth, while the EPA fish oil offers the necessary extra fat and omega-3 fatty acids. The Ultra Probiotic Powder and yogurt provide all the beneficial bacteria for normal, healthy digestion. Be sure to mix well and serve the mixture at room temperature.

WEEK FIVE TO ADULTHOOD

Once a puppy reaches four weeks of age, other foods can be introduced. Start with the replacement milk mixture above, and then begin adding a bit of meat along with some cottage cheese or yogurt. As week five progresses add in tiny bits of beef kidney and heart, canned mackerel, a small bit of liver, and some egg (both yolk and white).

Next you can introduce chicken necks. I remove the skin and cut the necks into smaller pieces; the size of the pieces will depend on the size of your puppy. For toy breeds, necks can be ground (though you can leave some of the necks whole for recreational chewing).

Later in the week try introducing chicken wings. As with other meat with bones, the smaller the dog the more pieces you should cut their meal into—for larger puppies I cut the wings into two pieces, for medium-sized breeds, into four pieces, and so on. Pork neck bones—always very chewable and entertaining for puppies—are another good option around this age.

Keep the Milk Going!

Once other foods have been added to the puppies' diet the mother may refuse to clean stools. Don't worry—this is perfectly normal!

If the mother is still willing to nurse after the first four weeks it's important to let her—her milk is still the perfect food for your puppy and the best addition to the weaning diet.

If you want to encourage the mother to continue nursing, trim the puppies' nails.

How Much and How Often Should I Feed My Weaning Puppy?

After their first four weeks I generally offer puppies four or five meals per day—two main meals of RMBs and red meat and smaller snack meals of goat's milk, yogurt, eggs, and cottage cheese.

Puppies need to be fed about ten percent of their body weight until they've finished their quickest growth stages. For large and giant breeds this can take anywhere from twelve to eighteen months; for toy breeds, as few as six. Once their growth starts to slow down they'll transition to the normal adult food quantities—two to three percent of their body

> Offer very young puppies three to four meals a day, and then reduce the number of meals after they're finished teething (usually after six to seven months).

weight daily—and you should be able to transition your dogs to two meals a day (though toy breeds, with their higher metabolism, might do better on three or four).

During the rapid growth phase a ten-pound puppy would be eating just over a pound of food per day, which would break down into four meals—two main meals a day of meat and RMB and two snack meals of goat's milk, egg, and yogurt. Make sure to mix all the meals well and serve them at room temperature.

To take the guesswork out of feeding your puppies, let's take a look at some sample diets:

Sample Weaning Puppy Diet

Meal 1
  2 ounces goat's milk (fresh or canned)
  1 whole egg (yolk and white, no shell)
  1 tablespoon whole-milk yogurt

Meal 2
  2 (¼ cup) ounces ground beef, liver, sliced beef heart, kidney,
    or gizzards
  1 tablespoon whole-milk yogurt

Meal 3
  2 ounces goat's milk (fresh or canned)
  1 egg
  1 tablespoon whole-milk yogurt

Meal 4

    3 to 5 chicken necks or 2 to 3 chicken wings

Meal 5 (Bedtime or Play)

    Pork neck bones or beef or lamb ribs.

You can also substitute mackerel, salmon, or sardines in the weaning puppy's diet once or twice a week. As with the adult diet, organ meat should make up ten percent of what they eat; use mostly kidney (beef, pork, or lamb) with some slices of liver.

Though it's not essential, you can add one or two tablespoons of ground or pureed vegetables if you like (though make sure they make up less than one-sixth of the diet). Good choices include dark leafy greens, zucchini, broccoli, and cabbage. You can also use some carrots, squash, cauliflower, or canned pumpkin in a pinch. Mix the meat and vegetables well.

Transitioning to the Adult Diet

When your puppy reaches three or four months of age you can start to phase out the milk and egg meals. Begin by cutting down the two milk and egg meals to one (though it's a good idea to still add the egg from the first meal to the meat and vegetable meals you're feeding). The second milk meal can be phased out around the time the puppy is five or six months old.

Percentage of RMBs for Calcium and Variety

The two most important balancing factors in the puppy's diet are RMBs, which help balance the calcium and phosphorous levels, and variety. Like the adult dog, your puppy should be getting a good selection of meats (red meat, poultry, fish, and organ meat), eggs, vegetables, and dairy.

And while RMBs are the best source of calcium for your growing puppy, make sure that they only make up between forty and fifty per-

cent of the diet. Too much calcium, as we know, can be more dangerous than not enough.

Changing Your Puppy's Diet from Commercial to Homemade

The first time many of us see our new
puppy is after they've been whelped and
reared. Chances are once you get your
new friend home that you'll want to raise
him or her on a different diet than the
one he or she is used to. To ease the transition, remember these simple rules:

> If you're not feeding
> RMBs, supplement with
> about 900 milligrams of
> calcium carbonate per
> pound of food served.

KEEP IT SIMPLE!

Start out with small, frequent meals. Most puppies do fine with a complete, quick switch to a homemade diet, but some puppies may not
know what to do with fresh food. Try mixing the meat, yogurt, and
eggs with kibble to start.

WATCH FOR SIGNS!

It's important to do what you're comfortable with and what seems to
work best for your puppy. Note how he or she responds to the change
in diet and pace the transition accordingly.

DON'T STRESS!

Make mealtimes as stress-free as possible and try to keep the feeding
times consistent. Don't get upset if your dog doesn't seem interested
in the new food. Just pick the bowl up, walk away and try again later.
He or she will come around!

RMBS FOR PUPS!

Be sure to feed RMBs separately rather than with the kibble. Some
puppies may be delighted to get RMBs, while others may need to start

on ground or cut-up pieces. You can try cutting the meat with meat scissors or a meat cleaver, or you can even pound the RMBs with a hammer to help break them up in the beginning.

NOT TOO COLD!

Many puppies are sensitive to texture and temperature. Try to serve food as close to room temperature as you can.

AFTER MEAL BREAK!

Always remember that puppies need to eliminate after eating and often like to take a nap after their meal and potty break.

Berte's Zymes can be helpful for transitioning a puppy raised on kibble to a homemade diet. Give small and medium-sized puppies one-quarter of a tablet and large puppies half a tablet with their main meals.

Upset Stomach?

When you change your puppy's diet there's always the risk of gastric upset. Tummy upsets are common and are usually nothing to worry about. The first thing you should try is to fast the puppy for a few hours before reintroducing the meals in smaller portions. Be sure to lower the fat of the meals you feed during this time too—along with overfeeding, an excess of fat in the diet is one of the main causes of gastric upset.

If problems persist take your dog to the vet, who can rule out more serious problems and do a fecal check to make sure parasites aren't the cause.

Most of the time the cause is a simple one and nothing to be concerned about. Often you can treat it at home by adding settling foods to the diet. If your puppy has diarrhea or is vomiting, there are a couple of excellent home remedies you can try.

Diarrhea Remedy

Overeating is the most common cause of diarrhea. Try giving your puppy some plain canned pumpkin to help him or her form firm stools—half a teaspoon for dogs weighing up to thirty pounds, one teaspoon for dogs weight thirty to sixty pounds, and two teaspoons to one tablespoon for larger dogs.

Vomiting Remedy

Cabbage is great for settling a troubled stomach. Boil some cabbage for about fifteen to twenty minutes, let it cool, then give half a teaspoon per ten pounds of body weight as needed.

Protein and Your Puppy

Puppies grow at an astounding rate, and protein helps them do it. Animal proteins are the building blocks of your puppy's growing body and they need plenty in their diets to form healthy muscles, skin, coat, and bones. Sound simple? It hasn't always been. The matter of protein in a puppy's diet has been a thorny and controversial one for some time among dog lovers. For a long time protein was thought to cause joint problems in dogs, particularly in large breeds. In more recent times, a considerable body of research has suggested the opposite— that puppies, even more so than adults, need a high amount of animal protein to grow properly and can't really have too much.

Research done at the Purina Pet Care Center has revealed how important a high level of protein is in helping puppies grow and stay free of illness. In one study, puppies fed a low-protein diet showed signs of stunted growth compared to dogs who got higher amounts of protein. When the stunted puppies were changed to a high-protein diet, they began to grow normally.[1] Other studies of large-breed puppies have shown that raising them on high-protein diets enables them to grow up healthy and strong without any of the problems such diets were thought to have caused.

Puppies should always be fed more than fifteen percent protein to ensure they grow up to become healthy adults.[2] And as with any dog, big or small, young or old, the golden rule of feeding protein is that quality rather than quantity makes all the difference. Use the best quality animal proteins you can find, which will allow you to feed your dog in healthy amounts. Overfeeding—a common problem when feeding poor sources of protein—can cause a whole host of problems in a puppy from arthritis to orthopedic issues.

Supplements

Supplements are very important for a strong and healthy puppy, providing a broad spectrum of essential nutrients that are sometimes difficult to provide in the diet in complete amounts. Try adding the following supplements to your puppies' weaning diet:

- Berte's Daily Blend helps puppies metabolize the calcium in their diets. Puppies find the powder delicious and it's a cinch to mix with food. Small and medium breed puppies get a quarter of a teaspoon and large breed puppies half a teaspoon, both twice a day.
- Berte's Green Blend provides the additional minerals and phytonutrients puppies need. Small and medium breed puppies get an eighth of a teaspoon and large breed puppies a quarter of a teaspoon, both twice a day.
- Berte's Ultra Probiotic Powder offers a good supply of beneficial digestive bacteria and keeps your puppy's stools firm. Give a quarter of a teaspoon for small to medium breed puppies and half a teaspoon for large breed puppies, both twice a day.
- Give one 1,000-milligram capsule of EPA Fish Oil daily per ten to twenty pounds of body weight to ensure proper brain and nerve development and a healthy skin and coat.

In a Nutshell

When you consider everything together it can seem like there's a lot to remember when feeding your puppy. It's not so complicated, though. To keep feeding your growing dog simple and stress free, just remember:

USE HIGH QUALITY PROTEINS, AND LOTS OF THEM

If you're feeding your puppy processed food, then look for a premium brand that uses good quality protein. If you're feeding a homemade diet, whether raw or cooked, vary the animal proteins as much as possible.

KEEP PUPPIES AND GROWING DOGS LEAN

Overweight and obese dogs have a much higher chance of developing serious health problems, so avoid feeding your dog too much.

DON'T GO OVERBOARD WITH CALCIUM

Be aware of the calcium requirements for the different kinds of diets in this chapter and, as always, be careful not to give your dog too much.

BE FLEXIBLE!

Each puppy is different, so it's important to be flexible with your puppy's meals. The amount of food he or she needs depends on his or her current stage of growth. Always remember, like human children, puppies' tastes will vary. Some puppies might love vegetables while others will turn their noses up at them. Watch your puppy closely for clues to what he or she wants and needs.

Cover all these bases and you'll soon have the joy of seeing your puppy grow into a healthy adult dog that is full of energy. (For more information on cooking for your dog, see "Chapter Eight: Feeding Homemade Diets the Easy Way," "Chapter Nine: Feeding Raw the Easy Way," and "Chapter Ten: Feeding Cooked Diets the Easy Way.")

Chapter Thirteen

Feeding Senior Dogs

Demystifying Senior Canine Nutrition

So now we know how to feed our puppies and adult dogs, what do we do when they start getting older? If you ask around, it's hard not to be confused by the conflicting advice out there. Some sources tell us that older dogs need less protein and more carbohydrates, while others say their diet should stay pretty much the same. The pet companies, for their part, will tell you that older dogs can't handle too much protein and need a diet high in fiber and low in fat to fight the obesity so common in dogs their age. In short, they need the commercial "senior" formulas.

Like so many commercially available diets, these "senior" formulas wind up having the opposite effect than what is intended—the dog lacks the satisfaction of the high-protein, high-fat diet she craves and ends up constantly hungry and begging for food. The high fiber content combined with the low levels of protein end up damaging her coat, skin, and organs without producing any real results in terms of weight loss. So what's the solution?

A truly supportive senior diet is much different than the formulas you'll find on the shelves of your local supermarkets and much closer to the puppy and adult diets we've looked at already—a diet high in fresh animal protein and low in carbohydrates. There's no radical change in diet required. If you want to keep your older dog trim, happy, and healthy, there are just a few simple rules to remember:

DON'T SKIMP ON THE PROTEIN!

Older dogs can't process protein as well as they used to so they need more to make up for it. Offer a variety of high-quality animal proteins like beef, lamb, fish, pork, dairy products, and eggs.

IF YOUR DOG IS OVERWEIGHT, CUT THE FAT

Use low-fat yogurt and cottage cheese in place of whole-milk dairy products and switch from fattier meats like lamb and pork to leaner options like chicken and beef. Try trimming some of the fat from the meat you serve, and drain any excess off after cooking.

REDUCE CARBOHYDRATES IN THE DIET

Eliminate starchy or high-glycemic foods like potatoes, sweet potatoes, carrots, and green peas, and avoid rice and grains.

Protein for Seniors

The subject of protein in senior diets has provoked a lot of debate over the years, with the common wisdom of yesteryear to reduce the protein in senior diets now giving way to the realization that protein is key to maintaining an aging dog's health and should not be reduced at any stage in the dog's life.

A diet lacking in protein can cause a whole host of problems ranging from loss of lean body mass and lethargy to an impaired immune system and hypersensitivity to drugs.[3] A lot of the old thinking about senior dogs and protein was based upon the belief that dogs just couldn't physically metabolize, or process, excess protein. But recent studies have dispelled this myth, confirming that high quality protein is still the key to a healthy dog.

But Don't Older Dogs with Kidney Problems Need Less Protein?

This is another persistent myth. Recent studies have confirmed that dogs with renal problems need a high level of protein to maintain organ health and integrity, and that high-protein diets have no negative effects on their bodies or kidneys.

Still, if you feel your senior dog might have some kidney problems, always check with your vet. (For more information on diets for dogs with kidney problems, see "Chapter Twenty-One: Diets for Kidney Needs.")

Supplements for Seniors

The twilight years of a dog's life should be some of his or her happiest. To ensure that they are, try these supplements:

- EPA fish oil helps senior dogs maintain cognitive function while protecting the liver and kidneys. The omega-3 also keeps their skin and coat healthy and shiny.
- Berte's Immune Blend contains lots of antioxidants and helps protect the kidneys and nerves. For healthy seniors use a half dose.

Chapter Fourteen

Diet and Pregnancy

For Healthy Pups, Get the Diet Right

As any breeder or mother will tell you, it's hard to overstate the importance of good nutrition during pregnancy. And while the pressure of home-feeding an expectant mother can seem daunting at first, don't fear—ensuring the fertility of the mother and the health of her whelps is simpler than you think. With the right combination of diet, supplements, and exercise you'll have a happy mother and a healthy brood in no time.

By far the most important factor in a successful pregnancy is diet, one that offers her variety while accounting for her many and varied nutritional needs. First and foremost the diet of the brood bitch needs to be rich in high-quality protein while providing all the calcium she needs. If you're feeding raw, satisfying both these needs won't be a problem. If you're feeding a commercial dog food, though, this is the time to consider adding some fresh food to the diet.

A lactating female requires even more food than those who are pregnant. Keep her diet high in animal protein (to help with milk production) and fat (to ensure she has enough energy for labor and lactation). She will burn more calories at this point than any other.

Good protein sources for expectant mothers are raw meats like ground beef, beef heart, kidney, lamb, pork, and poultry, along with raw eggs and dairy sources such as yogurt, goat's milk, and cottage cheese, all of which offer not only plenty of protein, but also fat, iron, minerals, and vitamins. Protein is essential for building the baby pup's tissues, while fat offers the mother the extra energy she needs to get through the rigors of pregnancy.

Do Expectant Mothers Need More Food?

They sure do. A normal healthy adult female canine should be eating two to three percent of her body weight each day, but a pregnant bitch will require significantly more than that to keep up with the demands on her body. Most bitches will require about a third more food after the fourth week, with this amount increasing as the whelping date nears. Vary the amount you feed according to the litter size. If she's carrying a large litter, try feeding smaller more frequent meals to accommodate the decreasing room in her abdomen.

Can I Feed the Same Foods as Usual?

In a word, yes. The easiest way to ensure a healthy pregnancy and a happy brood is to feed a varied diet rich in high-quality proteins, as you would normally. Her diet should always include animal proteins like muscle meat, beef kidney, canned fish like mackerel or salmon, as well as eggs, yogurt, and goat's milk.

Minerals and Supplements During Pregnancy

While a raw diet is the closest thing to optimum nutrition you can offer your brood bitch, because of her needs during pregnancy there is no diet—whether homemade or commercial—that can satisfy all her nutritional requirements, making good supplements more important than ever.

OMEGA-3 FATTY ACIDS

This essential fatty acid, so important throughout your dog's life, is never more important than during pregnancy. It plays a crucial role in fetal brain and nerve development as well as helping with eyesight. It's also great for maintaining a healthy immune system. Try giving 1,000 milligrams (180 EPA and 120 DHA) per twenty pounds of the mother's body weight daily.

FOLATE

Folic Acid (also known as B9) helps prevent several birth defects involving neural tube, cleft palate and spinal defects. Try giving 400 micrograms for a large dog, 200 micrograms for a medium dog, and fifty micrograms for a smaller dog. Good dietary sources include pork, poultry, and liver, or you can try, like I do, giving your soon-to-be bred and pregnant girls cereal fortified with folic acid. It's important to make sure these girls get enough folic acid before pregnancy (introduce it at least two months before conception) as well as during fetal growth.

CALCIUM

The right calcium balance is vital not only for the fetus' bone and tooth development, but for the expectant mother herself, both during pregnancy and while she's nursing. If the bitch's diet is deficient her body will leech it from her bones to make sure the pup is still getting enough, putting her at risk of a whole host of problems. Be careful, too, of offering too much—an excess can cause it's own set of serious problems.

Berte's Daily Blend is a great addition to her diet and will help make sure she gets all the vitamins she needs, especially vitamin D.

Thankfully, the general rules for calcium supplementation hold true for pregnant bitches—if she's on a commercial diet or a diet consisting of at least forty percent RMB, she'll be getting enough calcium and you won't have to worry about supplementation. If you're offering a homemade (raw or cooked) diet without RMBs, be sure to add at least 900 milligrams of calcium per pound of food served.

IRON

Iron is essential for the production of red blood cells and the prevention of anemia. The best sources of iron are always meats like beef and beef hearts and organ meats like kidney and liver. Eggs are a great source, too.

DULCE

Dulce is high in iron, and along with other sea algaes can be useful in helping the mother's digestion during pregnancy.

VITAMIN C

Vitamin C helps with the uptake of iron into the system and collagen-building while supporting the immune system.

VITAMIN D

Vitamin D is important for the proper absorption of calcium. The best dietary sources include canned mackerel and salmon, eggs and dairy products.

WHELP HELP

This great product, available online, contains red raspberry and fennel, both of which help with the mother's milk production and ingestion as well as easing and speeding up the labor process. Use it during the last three weeks of pregnancy and then throughout lactation.

RESCUE AND RELIEF ESSENCE

Rescue and Relief Essence helps to calm your bitch during whelp if she gets stressed.

A VITAMIN TO AVOID

The one vitamin to avoid is vitamin A, which, if given in too high a dose, can cause damage the fetus in the first few weeks of pregnancy. So how can she get too much vitamin A? Feeding too much liver can raise her vitamin A to dangerous levels, as can the addition of cod liver oil to the diet. Keep the daily vitamin A dosage below 5,000 milligrams for large dogs, 2,000 milligrams for medium dogs, and 1,000 milligrams for small dogs.[4]

In a Nutshell

There are just a few crucial things to remember when feeding your expectant mother.

USE VARIETY!

Like human mothers, pregnant bitches are often drawn to new foods during pregnancy, foods that aren't usually their favorites. Often my girls will want more organ meat, dairy, and RMBs. Follow her lead and offer her a variety of food types, feeding her what she's attracted to while making sure her diet is balanced.

KEEP HER IN SHAPE!

It's vital for the pregnant mother to stay in good physical shape throughout the pregnancy. Take her on daily walks and give her plenty of time in the yard and lots of low-impact exercise. She'll thank you for it when it's time to whelp!

FEED HER MORE!

She'll need a lot more food than normal during the pregnancy. Start to feed her around a third more food after the fourth week, increasing this even more towards whelping time.

SUPPLEMENT!

Be sure to supplement her diet with omega-3 fatty acids, folic acid, and vitamin C, as it's difficult to provide enough of these essential nutrients through diet alone.

DON'T FRET!

Despite the fear you might have initially about taking diet and nutrition into your own hands at such an important time as pregnancy, it won't be long before you see how strong and healthy a custom-prepared homemade diet makes the bitch and her brood. And it's not so hard—most of the rules for pregnant feeding you already know; others you just have to alter a bit. Chances are you'll soon find it very satisfying to take your pregnant dog's nutrition into your own hands, ensuring her health and longevity—and some busy years to come!

Chapter Fifteen

Feeding on the Go

Frequent Flyers

Many of our dogs are frequent travelers, trekking around the country with us on vacations or heading off with professional handlers to dog shows and events. And as anyone who's ever traveled with a dog knows, feeding on the go can be tricky. But it doesn't have to be. As long as you're prepared, you can keep your dog in great shape wherever you happen to go.

Traveling with a Homemade Diet

If you're thinking that feeding a raw or homemade diet on the road seems like too much and you might just go back to kibble for the trip, stop! Giving your dog a diet she's used to helps calm her during the stresses of travel. As for your stress, there's no need to worry—if you've got all the things you need it's a simple matter of lunch and dinner.

What You'll Need

Aside from food, there's a few essential things you'll need for your trip, including:

- A cooler (one you can add ice to, or one you can plug into a car or regular outlet)
- Zip-lock bags
- Small plastic garbage bags (for cleaning up)
- Paper towels
- Utensils (for cutting and mixing your dog's food)

You know by now not to fret too much about balancing the nutrients in every meal. Just make sure your dog has a variety of fresh foods over the course of the trip and that you add some supplements to each meal.

When you're traveling with a cooler it's easy: just pack meal-size portions of your dog's favorite meaty bones—chicken necks and backs, say, or pork neck bones—into individual freezer bags and freeze them in advance. These RMB meals will keep in the cooler for two or three days.

The beauty of feeding a homemade diet is that most of the foods you normally feed your dog can be readily found wherever you go, making it easy to offer a healthy, consistent diet.

No matter what diet your dog is on, bring along either bottled water or water from home if you can, as changes in water can cause digestive upsets.

If you're going on a long journey you can pick up more RMBs at any supermarket, so be sure to make a note of where the local grocery stores are in the town or city you're visiting. For your other meals you can alternate between ground beef and another red meat you've either got packed or that you've picked up at the supermarket.

For dogs on a cooked diet, don't forget about the canned meal you can provide, too! Try feeding canned mackerel or salmon mixed with either plain canned pumpkin or mixed vegetables.

Eggs, whole-milk yogurt, and cottage cheese can also easily be added for variety during a road trip.

If you can, bring your dog's food and water bowls from home and try to maintain your usual meal schedule. By keeping a routine and bringing a few comforts from home you can help alleviate some of the stresses of traveling.

Traveling with Kibble

If your dog eats a commercial kibble diet, the main thing to remember is to make sure you've got plenty of the same brand of dog food for the duration of the trip. Always be sure to keep the dry food in well-sealed containers for long road trips so it doesn't come into contact with dirt and moisture.

Handy Travel Supplements and First Aid Items

Because it can be difficult to feed everything you usually do at home, supplements can come in very handy when you're traveling. And because you never know what might happen, a well-stocked canine first aid kit is a must for any trip with your dog. Here are a few things that can help keep your dog happy and healthy during the most stressful of journeys:

BERTE'S IMMUNE BLEND

This liver-flavored, vitamin-packed supplement helps keep the immune system strong during times of stress. It comes in powdered form in an unbreakable plastic container, making it super convenient. It's also a very handy all-in-one supplement to use while your dog is at a boarding kennel or on the road with a dog show handler.

TASHA'S TUMMY TRAVELER FORMULA

This alcohol-free herbal tincture contains ginger, chamomile, peppermint, and meadowsweet and helps to fight nausea, settle the stomach, and reduce anxiety and motion sickness. Give your dog a few drops twenty minutes before traveling and repeat in four hours if necessary.

BERTE'S GREEN BLEND

This yeast-free blend of sea vegetation is another great all-around supplement for traveling, offering a wide spectrum of nutrients it might be difficult to otherwise provide during your journey.

THAYER'S WITCH HAZEL WITH ALOE

A great formula to have on hand for hot spots, itchiness, ear problems, and minor scrapes and cuts. The witch hazel helps to stop itching while the aloe helps to cool and heal the area. It comes in an unbreakable plastic squirt bottle for easy application.

RESCUE AND RELIEF ESSENCE

This is a must-have item for any canine first aid kit. It's great for soothing the effects of any sudden trauma, stress, or panic, and can also come in handy during the onset of an illness. Rescue and Relief Essence can be applied in the mouth with the handy dropper top, on the skin (in areas like the ear leather), or added to the drinking water.

HALO DERMA DREAM

A great salve for irritation and wounds.

LAVENDER OIL

Apply a few drops of this essential oil to the tummy to reduce anxiety.

WILLOW BARK FORMULA

This great herbal tincture helps relieve inflammation, pain, and discomfort. Use only with food.

Chapter Sixteen

Working Dog Diets

All-Stars on a Junk Food Diet

Imagine, if you will, a professional athlete. He wakes up in the morning, does his stretches and prepares for a day of training. Before he heads out onto the track he sits down to a meal of processed food, his first of two for the day. Imagine that the food is cooked for three days using inferior-grade food products and then baked into small chunks, with supplements added as an afterthought. Notice something wrong with this picture? Would you expect this athlete to deliver his best performance on the field? Would this diet provide him with the nutrition he needs to compete at his best? Of course it wouldn't. So how do we expect our high-performance working dogs—our canine athletes—to put up with this treatment and still perform at their best?

Keeping the Engine Running

Dogs, as we know, depend on proteins and fats for energy and life-sustaining nutrients. Whereas human high-performance diets can get ridiculously complicated, the equation for working dogs is simple: the more energy they expend, the more animal fat and protein they need. And not only does such a diet keep them going, new research shows that diets high in fat and protein and low in carbohydrates actually increase performance.[5] Diets lacking in fats and protein, on the other hand, quickly affect the working dogs' stamina, causing them to become enervated; over time, serious health problems can develop.

Digestion takes up most of the energy in any living being. The less time a working dog spends digesting the more their energy can be put to better use, like in the field or the ring. If food is digested quickly, as is the case with animal fats and proteins, the working dog will not have to carry a full belly of food on to the field, giving the dog the energy he or she needs for working, and also lessening the chance of bloat or torsion. Carbohydrate-rich dry dog foods, the staple diet of most dogs, are difficult to digest and can tire a dog out, an undesirable situation for any dog let alone one who has to perform.

Up the Protein and Fat!

Protein not only provides energy and increases performance, it's important for preventing injuries, too. In a recent study, dogs undergoing rigorous training were given different amounts of protein. The dogs fed a lower-protein diet sustained many more injuries; in some cases, they had to stop training. The dogs on a high-protein diet, on the other hand, trained without problems or injuries. The study found that if all of the available protein is used for energy, as in the case of the dogs on low-protein diets, the body is robbed of the protein it needs to perform its other important functions, like repairing tissue and producing hormones. For working dogs, whose tissues are constantly being repaired, a high level of protein crucial.[6] Protein has also been found to reduce the risk of training anemia.

If your dog is competing in endurance sports, fat should account for between fifty and seventy percent of the diet. Source: www.livescience.com/animals/080925-sled-dogs.html

Fats, not carbohydrates, are the working dog's best energy source. Dogs find fats delicious and highly digestible, and unlike carbohydrates, they help keep energy levels stable. And there's no better source of the calories your working dog relies on than fats.[7]

Fluids

Feeding a high-fat diet will help keep your dog hydrated, but don't forget to give her or him a lot of water, too.[8] It's hard to overstate the importance of providing fresh water for your dog around the clock. Always bring buckets, spray bottles, water, and ice to any performance event, whatever the weather.

So What Do I Feed Then?

If you do some research, you'll quickly find that that the topic of carbohydrates in working dog diets is a controversial and touchy one. Pet food companies, it seems, have a vested interest in maintaining the myth that carbohydrates are necessary for our high-performance pets. In reality, a working dog's diet would be made up of forty percent protein and up to fifty percent fat, leaving little room for carbohydrates. This kind of diet, unfortunately, cannot be found on the market. But, as we're about to see, making a diet higher in fat and protein at home couldn't be simpler.

Transitioning

If your working dog has been on a kibble diet for a long time and you're worried that too quick a transition might affect his or her performance, an easy way to start feeding fresh foods is to mix them with your dry dog food. Start slowly, increasing the fresh ingredients over a six-week period. If you're confident that your dog will take to a more natural diet, you can simply switch her or him over to a raw diet directly. As always, just do what you feel comfortable with. A book on raw feeding and a mentor who knows the ropes always help, too.

Staples

The staples of a performance dog's raw diet should be RMBs, muscle meat, and organ meat, which together offer the protein, fat, moisture, and minerals your dog needs to be at his or her best.

You can leave carbohydrates out entirely or give a small amount of low-glycemic vegetables.

Figure 16.1. Foods That Are Particularly Well Suited to the Working Dog.	
RMBs	**Muscle Meat**
Chicken necks, backs, wings, leg quarters	Beef heart
Pork neck bones and ribs	Ground beef
Beef ribs and necks	Pork
Turkey necks (cut into four pieces)	Tripe
Rabbit	Lamb (very high in fat)
	Venison (a leaner option)
	Canned mackerel or salmon
	Buffalo
Organ Meat	**Other Animal Protein Sources**
Beef kidney and liver	Eggs
Lamb kidney and liver	Whole-milk yogurt
Pork kidney and liver	Cottage cheese
Fats	**Vegetables**
1,000 milligrams EPA fish oil	Pulped, pulverized or steamed:
Fish oils	Broccoli
	Dark leafy greens
	Celery
	Zucchini
	Cabbage

Sample Working Dog Diet

Morning or Noon

> Egg
> Yogurt or cottage cheese
> Muscle or organ meat
> Vitamin E (400 IU per fifty pounds of body weight)

Vitamin C (500 milligrams per 25 pounds of body weight)

B complex (25 milligrams per 50 pounds of body weight)

A few tablespoons of vegetables (optional)

A small amount of Berte's Green Blend (optional)

Salmon oil (1,000 milligrams per 20 pounds of body weight)

Evening

RMBs

Salmon oil (1,000 milligrams per 20 pounds of body weight)

Do Working Dogs Need More Food?

Working dogs still only need around two to three percent of their body weight in food per day, though more if your dog is lean and less if he or she is overweight. If you're unsure, just check the dog's ribs—if you have to dig for them the dog is too fat, and if you can see them the dog is too thin.

Supplements for Working Dogs

Giving your working dogs the right vitamins and supplements can help give them that extra edge they need to perform at their best while also ensuring their long-term health.

- Salmon oil or fish oil for energy and to fight inflammation
- Vitamin C for its collagen-building properties and antioxidant value
- Vitamin E to help with healing
- B complex for nerve and brain functions
- Digestive enzymes and Berte's Probiotic Powder to replace some of the beneficial bacteria working dogs can lose through stress
- Flexile Plus to help protect the joints
- Berte's Immune Blend to help maintain muscle integrity

Chapter Seventeen

Why Your Dog Is Not a Vegetarian

I'll Have the Tofu, Fido Will Have the Steak

While searching for information on the best canine diets, you'll no doubt find a lot of articles written in the last few years on vegetarian and vegan diets for dogs. What's interesting to note about almost all of these diets is their alarming similarity to the vegetarian diets recommended for people—they're high in grains, suggest using lots of vegetables, and sing the praises of tofu and soy products.

While a vegetarian diet is something you might happily choose for yourself, making the same choice for your dog is quite a different matter, and one that can have some potentially dangerous consequences. As we learned in the second chapter, humans and dogs are very different anatomically, and it's a mistake to impose one's diet on the other. Can you imagine people eating dog food?

Humans are omnivorous, and everything about us—our teeth, digestive tracts, even our saliva—is designed to help us break down plants. While we have also adapted to eating other kinds of food like meat and fats, the same cannot be said for dogs, who remain simple carnivores, with bodies unsure of what to do with the simplest salad or piece of toast. Dogs, as we know, are fundamentally different from us, with a digestive system designed solely for meats and fats. A tofu-based diet, however environmentally friendly, just won't cut it with dogs.

The Beef on Vegetarian Pets

A recent study of vegetarian dogs in Europe highlighted the dangers of canine vegetarian diets. In its sample group of vegetarian dogs, it found:

- Protein intake was inadequate for more than half of the dogs
- Calcium requirements were not met in sixty-two percent of the dogs' diets
- Phosphorus requirements were not met in approximately half the dogs
- Seventy-three percent of the dogs had an insufficient intake of sodium
- A high number of blood samples taken showed insufficient amounts of iron, copper, zinc, iodine, and vitamin D
- Fifty-six percent of the dogs were not getting enough vitamin B12

Even the commercial vegetarian diets tested lacked the nutrition necessary to keep a dog strong and healthy, the study found.[9] So why exactly is a vegetarian diet so lacking in what dogs need?

Dogs Need Meat!

Protein, so essential for healthy organs, skin, and growth, is comprised of different amino acids, each of them doing a specific job, and all of them working together to keep the body healthy. Dogs, as carnivores, need even more amino acids than humans and in different amounts.

As proponents of vegetarian diets rightly point out, combining certain vegetables and grains can provide most of the essential amino acids a *human* needs. The same anthropomorphic leap in logic that has allowed many people to think that dogs need carbohydrates has happened with vegetarian diets.

Carbohydrates are fattening to dogs, which is another dilemma with vegetarian diets: if you feed your dog a carbohydrate-based vegetarian diet, far more food will be needed for your dog to get all the protein he or she needs. Feeding this amount of food inevitably leads to gastric upsets and big, smelly stools, as well as heightening the risk of obesity.

Furthermore, dogs are very different beasts than humans and need some amino acids that are only readily available in animal sources, like taurine and l-carnitine, which help with heart function.[10] Tests have shown some dogs fed purely vegetarian diets are abnormally low in taurine, a deficiency that can lead to serious heart conditions like DCM (dilated cardiomyopathy). Add to that the fact that dogs can't digest plant proteins very well to begin with and it seems that no matter how you combine grains and vegetables, no matter how complex and well-thought out your vegetarian diet may seem, it won't provide your dog with everything he or she needs.[11]

Soy Protein

Although soy is a common staple of human vegetarian diets, it's a much more questionable inclusion in your dog's bowl. Soy is not a complete protein and is a common allergen for dogs to boot. Replacing animal protein with protein from soy products, however well it might work in a human diet, is definitely not recommended for your pet. A recent survey of dogs fed a vegetarian diet found that the few dogs who did not eat soy were in much better health than those who did.[12]

While there are a lot of sound environmental arguments that support the use of soy products in place of meat, when it comes to matters of anatomy it seems the canine just isn't cut out for the vegetarian lifestyle.

Minerals

While plants can be rich sources of minerals in our diets, they are incomplete sources for our pets. Plants can certainly offer some things your dog needs—many plants are high in phosphorus, potassium, and magnesium, for example—but they are particularly poor sources of sodium and calcium, as well as being high in phytates, which block the absorption of many important minerals. Although the pet food industry has been aware of this since the early 1980s, rather than reduce the amount of grains and starches in their commercial products they opted instead to add more calcium, zinc, magnesium, and iron.

If you were to feed a vegetarian or vegan diet to your dog you'd need to supplement calcium, zinc, magnesium, iron, and iodine to even get close to maintaining a healthy mineral balance. Adding minerals can be a tricky business. As we've learned, giving too much, or in the wrong combinations, can be just as dangerous as any deficiency. Needless to say, getting the mineral balance right in a vegetarian or vegan diet would be tough work indeed.

Vitamins

Vitamins, as we've seen, are an essential part of the canine diet. So, you might ask, if my dog was a vegan or vegetarian, would she get all the vitamins she needs? The short answer, I'm afraid, is no.

The vitamin A we find in plant sources is beta-carotene, and it has to go through a process of digestive conversion that dogs and cats are particularly ill equipped for. A canine diet needs at least some animal protein for your dog to get all the vitamin A she needs.

The richest sources of B vitamins are animal proteins, too. In the case of B2 (riboflavin)—the best sources of which are organ meats and dairy products—deficiencies can lead to stunted growth and heart failure.[13]

Tests have shown lower levels of vitamin D in the blood plasma of dogs fed a vegetarian diet, posing serious risks to normal, healthy development.[14]

In a Nutshell

Most vets will tell you that it's actually impossible to feed a vegan or vegetarian diet and still offer your dog all the nutrition he or she needs.

The sources out there that support canine vegetarian diets stress, at the same time, the complexity of supplying all the necessary nutrients and the dangers of leaving any out. The more reasonable sites recommend feeding at least eggs and dairy, even if your dog does without meat.

No one should attempt to feed a vegetarian diet to their dog without a thorough understanding of a dog's nutritional requirements and how those requirements can be met, including which supplements should be given and in what amounts. And no dog should be fed a vegan diet, which simply cannot meet a canine's nutritional needs.

Chapter Eighteen

Picky Eaters

Why Isn't My Dog Eating?

When your dog loses his or her appetite it's easy to feel frustrated and confused. Have I done something wrong? Is he or she depressed? Dogs can lose their appetite for a variety of reasons. Some are turned off of eating after convalescing from an illness, others because of certain medications. Natural bodily changes can affect the appetite, as well. Males for example, sometimes don't want to eat if a female in heat is within "scenting" range.

When your dog doesn't want to eat, it's a good idea to look for any changes in his or life that might be the cause. Have you moved recently? Has there been trouble at home? Stress is a common cause of appetite loss, and can often be caused by moving, changes in their owner's mood, weather patterns, or grief. Be sensitive to changes in the environment and how they affect your dog's health, as these can offer clues to why your dog is not eating and how you can get him or her back to the bowl again.

What Can I Do?

The first thing many people try to entice their pet back to the bowl is switching foods, often offering indulgent treats to whet their pet's appetite. While this can be effective, the first thing you should do if your dog experiences a serious loss of appetite is to head to the vet for a blood panel, urinalysis, and check-up. There are a number of health issues that can cause your dog to lose interest in food, and the first order of the day is to rule out any serious problems.

If the vet does discover something wrong, special diets or changes in the way you prepare your homemade meals may be able to help. A convalescing dog or one with ongoing health problems may need a few changes to tempt him or her back into eating. For some dogs it can be something as simple as a temperature adjustment, for others a change in texture or even a different bowl. Some animals may find hot foods more tempting, while others may prefer their food at room temperature. Many dogs like their food pureed or cut into smaller pieces, and some animals—especially those who are undergoing chemotherapy—may find the strong smell of a metal bowl turns them off.

(For more specific dietary advice for different health conditions, see "Part III: Remedial Diets Made Simple.")

Appetite-Inducing Foods

An effective technique with dogs that have lost their appetite is to offer them the foods most tempting to their palates—those high in fat. I've had some success with:

- Eggs lightly scrambled in butter with some yogurt or cream cheese
- Chicken liver sautéed in butter
- Hard-boiled eggs
- Cooked or boiled ground beef, mixed with grated or Parmesan cheese
- Baby foods, such as pureed meats
- Homemade chicken soup with noodles
- Canned salmon or sardines
- Macaroni and cheese with minced beef or sausage
- Plain yogurt with pureed liver (mix well!)
- Canned chicken chunks
- Bites from your own plate (dogs often think this is premium food!)

Be creative, but steer clear of highly spiced foods, which can cause tummy upsets. You should only use these foods for a few days, and they don't have to make up the whole meal—it's a good idea to mix them with the dog's regular diet to help enhance its flavor.

Trouble with Medications?

Some dogs, like us, are reluctant to take prescription pills or medications. Try coating these pills with cream cheese, peanut butter, Cheese Whiz or braunschweiger (soft luncheon meat) to make them go down easier.

My Dog Doesn't Like the New Diet!

As we've learned, you can switch a dog from a commercial diet to a home-cooked or raw one either gradually or, if you feel confident, all at once. If you make the switch to a raw diet too quickly, you might find your dog turning his or her nose up at the new food. Don't worry. Most often this has more to do with the temperature and texture of the food than with the food itself. Try feeding raw meals at room temperature rather than cold out of the refrigerator. Some dogs may prefer their new food in larger chunks, while others might take to it better if the meat is ground first.

Never give your dog frozen foods–they can't be digested.

If the foods are unfamiliar, it may take a bit of time and patience to get your dog to try them, and some time after that until they enjoy them. If a healthy dog shows no interest in what is offered, try removing the food after ten minutes and trying again at the next mealtime. Sometimes it helps to lightly heat up raw food, as the smell of fat can get a dog salivating!

Top Tips for Picky Eaters

When you have picky eaters on your hands, regardless of the food you're trying to feed or the diet you're trying to switch them to, there's a number of simple things you can do to get them chowing down:

DON'T HOVER!

Don't hover over the dog anxiously, waiting to see if he'll eat. Seeing how wound up mealtime makes you can often make the dog respond in kind and refuse to eat. Try to act nonchalant: just put the bowl down and turn away, or go into another room. If the dog won't eat it, take the food away and try again at the next meal. Sometimes we unwittingly teach our dogs not to eat through our own behavior!

KEEP IT REGULAR!

Try to feed the dog on a regular schedule and stick to it. That way they'll automatically become hungry at those times and anticipate their meal.

ACT HAPPY!

Act happy while preparing the meal, like dinnertime is an exciting event. If you have another dog that eats heartily, all the better—this will model competitive eating for the fussy dog, and should help him get into the food with more gusto. If the dog still won't eat, don't make a song and dance about it. Any stigma that surrounds eating can affect the dog's relationship to it later on, so try to stay clam and positive.

EXERCISE!

Giving your dog a regular exercise program can help promote appetite. This could be a daily walk, throwing a ball around, or going to the park. Agility, obedience, flyball, or tracking classes are great activities for any dog. Exercise helps build an appetite while offering the mental stimulation he or she may not get at home.

DON'T FRET—IT COULD BE NATURAL!

It's important not to get too worried about a dog's loss of appetite. There are plenty of natural changes a dog goes through that can cause changes in the way he or she eats. Some puppies, for instance, go through periods of fast growth before slowing down, so it's perfectly natural that there will be times when they'll eat less than they have been. The sore gums dogs get during teething can also cause a short-term loss of appetite, as can hormonal changes in intact females.

Part III

Remedial Diets
Made Simple

How To Use This Section

In the final section of this book we will examine specific nutritional needs for common canine health problems. While we will take a look at the symptoms, diagnosis, and treatment of different canine health conditions, the main focus will be on offering your dog the right nutrition for management and prevention of these problems.

The information contained in this chapter should only be used as a guide. Always be sure to have your pet examined and diagnosed by a veterinarian and follow his or her treatment instructions.

Chapter Nineteen

Heart-Healthy Diets

As a dog owner, it is important to have your veterinarian perform a wellness health checkup at least yearly and this is especially important for senior dogs. Heart problems are the second biggest cause of canine mortality, behind cancer. Heart issues most commonly affect older dogs but can strike at any age.[1] So what causes them, and what can we do?

In this section we will examine the different kinds of heart diseases and their treatments, followed by some simple advice on how you can best support your dog with good nutrition.

Diagnosis

Diagnosing heart disease can sometimes be perplexing. Symptoms can overlap, making it difficult to get a clear diagnosis. The first thing you should do when your dog is diagnosed with heart disease is ask your veterinarian these three questions:

- What type of heart disease does he or she have?
- What stage of the disease is he or she in?
- Is it progressive, meaning will it get worse?

The answers to these questions will help you get a handle on how serious the problem is and to what extent it can be managed at home. Changes in diet and lifestyle can make a big difference to a dog suffering from heart problems.

To find out the stage of heart disease that your dog is in, it's useful to know the four classes of heart disease:

Figure 19.1. Classifications of Heart Disease.[2]	
Class I	No limitations on physical activity. Activity doesn't cause symptoms.
Class II	Slight limitation of physical activity. Ordinary activity causes symptoms.
Class III	Marked limitation of physical activity. Symptoms occur with less than ordinary activity.
Class IV	Extreme limitation of physical activity. Symptoms present at rest.

The more serious your dog's heart problem is, the more drastic the changes you will have to make to his or her diet and lifestyle. If your dog is experiencing end-stage heart disease, for example, it would be appropriate to significantly reduce the sodium and protein in his or her diet, as we will discuss shortly. The diet of a dog with Class I or II heart disease would be much more similar to a normal diet.

Types of Heart Diseases

There are three areas of heart problems in dogs: those that affect the valves in the heart (heart murmurs), those that involve the heart muscle (myocardium), and those that arise from old age.

HEART MURMURS

Valve problems are the most common type of heart problems in canines and account for two thirds of the diagnosed conditions. Valvular problems are congenital, which means the dog was born with them, and they are characterized by heart murmurs.

There are many kinds of heart murmurs that range from mild to potentially fatal, so it's very important to have every puppy's heart checked by a veterinarian. (For a more definitive diagnosis have a cardiologist-board-certified veterinarian do the check up.)

Some murmurs, known as innocent murmurs, resolve themselves by the time the dog reaches about four months of age. If a murmur remains past that age, be sure to visit a veterinarian cardiologist for a proper diagnosis.

Signs of valvular problems include a lack of tolerance and enthusiasm for exercise, coughing (especially first thing in the morning or night), fainting, and weight loss.[3]

CARDIOMYOPATHY

Another common type of heart disorder is cardiomyopathy, which occurs when the dog's heart muscle is too thin. This illness usually arises due to infection, autoimmune disorders, or a nutritional deficiency, and generally affects large to giant breed dogs of young to middle age.

Symptoms include increased thirst and appetite, weight loss, fluid accumulation in the abdomen, and digestive problems. If you notice any of these problems, check for both hypothyroid conditions and a heart issue, as these symptoms are common to both disorders.[4]

Hypertrophic cardiomyopathy (HCM) is when the opposite happens, and the muscle walls of the heart thicken. Though more common in cats, it is also occasionally seen in dogs.[5]

OLD AGE

The final type of canine heart problem concerns older dogs. As dogs age, the arteries in the heart can begin to stiffen, causing problems with blood flow to the heart. Poor diets, particularly those lacking in iron, can also result in poor oxygen flow to the heart.

Treatment

No matter what your dog's diagnosis may be there are a number of things you can do to support his or her heart health through good nutrition and supplements. If you suspect your dog is suffering from a heart problem, take him or her to the vet, who will be able to tell you what heart condition your dog has and how serious it may be.

A thorough examination should test for other problems of the heart such as heartworms, tumors, bacterial infections, thyroid dysfunction, and autoimmune diseases, all of which can affect heart function.

Traditional Treatments for Heart Disease

Several prescription medications are used to help heart function, and it's important to know what each one does and what side effects each may cause.

Figure 19.2. Common Heart Medications for Canines.[6]		
Medication Type	What Does It Do?	Medications
Diuretics	Fights fluid build-up around the heart or abdomen.	Furosemide, spironolactone
Antihypertensive diuretics	Assists in dilating arteries and veins, helping the heart to pump blood more efficiently.	Enalapril, capoten, enacard, nitroglycerine
Digitalis glycosides	Increases the force of the heart's contractions. Monitor use of these carefully as the side effects can be toxic.	Foxaline, digitoxin, and lanoxin
Beta blockers	Useful in hypertrophic cardiomyopathy and dilated cardiomyopathy. Slows the heart rate, helping the ventricles fill with blood between contractions.	Atenolol and propanolol

If your dog is prone to edema (retaining water), hypertension (high blood pressure), or is currently taking a prescription medication, be sure to check with your vet about what changes you'll need to make.

In recent years many pet owners have started to complement the traditional pharmaceutical treatment of heart conditions with heart-supportive dietary supplementation. Made from natural ingredients, these supplements come without many of the side effects of conventional medicines. (See the section titled "Supplements," page 130, for more information.)

Diet

In most cases, the diet of a dog with heart problems won't be that much different from that of a healthy dog, but making a few minor changes and adding the right supplements can increase his or her chances of a longer, healthier life.

What to Feed

Fresh foods like meat, eggs, vegetables, and dairy are all suitable for dogs with heart problems, with raw foods being the most beneficial. Raw diets are naturally low in sodium and high in taurine, an amino acid that supports heart function, making them ideal, but home-cooked diets are great, too. If you're feeding a cooked or commercial diet, consider including some raw meat to make sure your dog gets all the taurine he or she needs.

It's a good idea to include organ meats, like beef kidney and liver, at least twice a week. (Be sure to use liver in smaller amounts, as it is very rich.) Heart is high in the amino acids needed for heart health (l-carnitine and taurine), so it's another great choice for dogs with cardiac disease. Try to feed heart at least twice a week.

Foods to Avoid

Avoid feeding high-sodium meats such as ham, bacon, and other smoked or cured meats. If your dog is overweight, or in class III or IV of heart disease, be sure to trim or drain excess fat when preparing the food, and if you're serving poultry be sure to remove the skin. Overweight dogs and those in the latter stages of heart disease should steer clear of high-fat foods in general (such as lamb and pork).

Sodium and Minerals

The first thing many people think of in when they hear the phrase "heart-healthy diet" is reduced-salt/sodium. While reducing dietary sodium is generally the first line of defense for humans suffering from heart disease, it's a different matter for dogs, whose salt intake should be determined by the severity of their condition.

Homemade diets are naturally low in sodium. Be careful with commercial diets, in which sodium is often added as a preservative.

Restricting sodium is likely unnecessary when your dog is in the early stages of heart disease. In fact, doing so may actually do more harm than good. Dogs in the later stages of heart disease, however, often do require significant reductions in dietary sodium and fat. As always, if you're unsure, check with your vet.

When starting your dog on heart disease medication, be sure to find out if and how the medication may affect your dog's nutritional needs. A number of drugs used to combat heart disease necessitate potassium supplementation, others require more magnesium and less potassium, and others require restricted sodium intake. Read the prescription inserts and follow your veterinarian's advice.

Protein and Fat

Protein is extremely important for dogs of all ages, shapes, and sizes, including those with heart disease. Unless your veterinarian tells you otherwise, never restrict protein in the diet of a dog suffering from heart problems, as protein starvation can make the situation worse, leading to stress on the heart and loss of muscle mass.

Be sure to use high-quality animal proteins, and serve them raw or only lightly cooked. Overcooking can destroy taurine and l-carnitine, two of the key nutrients needed for a healthy canine heart. Try offering l-carnitine-rich red meats, which support the heart's muscle cell integrity, especially if your dog is suffering from hypotrophic or hypertrophic cardiomyopathy.

Dogs suffering from heart problems should be fed a diet with only a moderate level of fat, especially if the dog is overweight or in the later stages of heart disease. While dogs don't have the same problems with cholesterol as humans do, being overweight can still put an extra burden on the heart, making it crucial to keep your dog at a normal, healthy weight.

Remember, feed these approximate amounts daily:

100-pound dog:	2–3 pounds daily, or two meals of 1–1.5 pounds each
75-pound dog:	1.5–2 pounds daily, or two meals of 12–18 ounces each
50-pound dog:	1–1.5 pounds daily, or two meals of 8–12 ounces each
25-pound dog:	8–12 ounces daily, or two meals of 4–6 ounces each

Sample Heart-Healthy Diets, Both Raw and Cooked

Here are sample heart-healthy diets, both raw and cooked, with quantities designed for a fifty-pound adult dog.

HEART-HEALTHY RAW DIET

Morning

6 ounces (¾ cup) meat, alternating beef heart, kidney, tripe, turkey, chicken, lamb, or rabbit

4 ounces (½ cup) pureed or steamed vegetables, including broccoli, zucchini, dark leafy greens, sweet potato, green beans, cabbage, and carrots

1 egg or 2 ounces plain yogurt

Combine the raw (or lightly cooked) meat with the fully cooked, mashed vegetables. When cool, mix in the yogurt and serve.

Evening

12 ounces (1½ cups) chicken necks or backs (remove the skin if your dog is overweight), or pork neck bones or tails, lamb breast, or turkey necks

HEART-HEALTHY COOKED DIET

Morning

> 6 ounces (¾ cup) cooked ground beef, beef heart, kidney, lamb, turkey, chicken, or rabbit (drain fat if dog is overweight)
>
> 1 egg, hard-boiled, soft-boiled, or scrambled, or 2 ounces plain yogurt
>
> 4 ounces (½ cup) steamed vegetables, including broccoli, zucchini, dark leafy greens, sweet potato, green beans, cabbage, and carrots
>
> 900 milligrams calcium carbonate or 1/4 teaspoon ground eggshell

> Mix the cooked meat, egg or yogurt, and vegetables together. Add the eggshell and stir to combine.

Evening

> Similar to the morning meal, but use a different meat source for variety.

Supplements

Supplements are becoming a popular complementary form of treatment for canines with heart disease. While they may not replace traditional therapies and medications, research has shown that these supplements can enhance heart function, improving a dog's quality of life while promoting longevity.

In addition to the supplements listed above, consider adding acidophilus or a probiotic blend, as well as digestive enzymes with pancreatin, to aid digestion.

Some supplements, like taurine and l-carnitine, can be supplemented or given in the form of animal protein. Whenever possible, offer the fresh protein source.

Monitor your dog's health condition in consultation with your veterinarian. This, along with diet and supplements, will offer your dog the best chance for longevity and improved quality of life.

Figure 19.3. Heart-Supportive Supplements.

Supplement	Sources	Benefits	Dosage
L-Carnitine	Animal proteins, including beef and pork (avoid over-cooking)	Stops cells in the heart muscle from deteriorating Aids in heart function Important for cardiomyopathy	500 milligrams daily per 20 pounds of body weight
Taurine	Animal proteins, including chicken, beef, and organ meat (avoid overcooking)	Important for proper heart function	If inadequate in the diet, add 500 milligrams daily per 50 pounds of body weight
COQ10 (enzyme)	Supplements	Helps support the heart Lowers blood pressure Antioxidant	About 1–2 milligrams daily per pound of body weight
Omega-3 fatty acids	Fish oil Salmon Oil	Controls inflammation Stops loss of muscle mass Supports the immune system, coat, skin, and hormone regulation	Approximately 1,000 milligrams (180 EPA, 120 DPA) daily per 10 pounds of body weight
Vitamin E (give with fish oil for best effect)	Supplements	Supports heart function Works synergistically with omega-3 fatty acids	Around 5 IU daily per pound of body weight
Vitamin B Complex	Supplements	Fights cardiomyopathy	A medium-sized dog would get a B-50 complex once or twice a day
Vitamin C	Supplements	Helps synthesize carnitine	For a medium-sized dog, 250–500 milligrams once or twice a day

Chapter Twenty

Diets for Dogs with Cancer

It's beyond the scope of this book to look at the many kinds of cancer and their various symptoms, diagnoses, and treatments. In this chapter, we'll look more generally at nutrition for dogs with cancer.

Effective Homemade Nutrition

Dogs diagnosed with cancer need all the help they can get, making good nutrition choices very important. In combination with veterinary treatment, a healthy and varied diet is a key factor in the recovery and quality of life for dogs fighting cancer. Offering the right fresh-food diet and supplements helps boost your dog's immune system while providing him or her with great tasting food.

Not surprisingly, studies on dogs have revealed that the best cancer-fighting diets are those low in carbohydrates and high in protein with significant levels of fat. These are very similar to the diets we have learned about so far. Studies have found that carbohydrates offer fuel for cancer cells and should be avoided, making most commercial diets off limits.

One of the most important things to remember when feeding a sick dog is that the best recipes are made with love and care. These ingredients offer as much healing power as the food itself.

To get started, let's take a look at the best foods and food types for fighting cancer. We will also examine the types of food that should be avoided.

Carbohydrates

For a dog with cancer, some carbohydrates are more "friendly" than others. The best of this group are the lower glycemic vegetables, which contain the least starch and sugar. To make things easier, here are some good vegetable carbohydrate options for your dog, along with the carbohydrates to avoid:

Figure 20.1. Vegetables for Dogs with Cancer.	
Good Choices	Avoid
Zucchini	Potatoes
Yellow crookneck squash	Yams
Pattypan squash	Carrots
Dark leafy greens	Green peas
Broccoli	Sweet potatoes
Cabbage	Hard rind squashes like winter squash
Brussels sprouts	All grains
Cauliflower	
Bok choy	

Protein

Like healthy dogs, dogs with cancer need quality animal proteins and a variety of them. Try to stick to the varied protein-rich meals we discussed in "Part II: Feeding Your Dog the Easy Way."

Fats

Dogs with cancer need a lot of good-quality fats, so offer fatty foods such as lamb, pork, eggs, and whole-milk yogurt. When you're feeding poultry, leave the skin on, and use the dark meat whenever possible as it has the highest fat content. Canned fish is also a good source of fat. Always use whole-milk cultured dairy products such as yogurt and cottage cheese, and continue to provide daily fish and fish oil supplements.

The Cancer-Starving Diet

For a diet with the best nutrition, try to feed a ratio of around forty percent protein, forty percent fat and twenty percent carbohydrates. If you are feeding a raw diet with RMBs, you can drop the amount of carbohydrates even further.

> The amount you feed shouldn't change. Dogs affected by cancer will still need meals that are two to three percent of their bodyweight daily.

In home-cooked diets, carbohydrates are added for their fiber content, which helps keep the stools firm. But in a raw diet with bones the RMBs do this job, so there's very little need for other carbohydrate sources. As with any diet for a sick dog, offer as much variety as possible to keep the dog's appetite stimulated.

The Raw Diet

Let's start by taking a look at the sample raw diet, which you might notice is not as specific as other diets mentioned so far. Choose the foods your dog likes best from those listed here, but always offer plenty of variety.

Remember, feed these approximate amounts daily:

100-pound dog:	2–3 pounds daily, or two meals of 1–1.5 pounds each
75-pound dog:	1.5–2 pounds daily, or two meals of 12–18 ounces each
50-pound dog:	1–1.5 pounds daily, or two meals of 8–12 ounces each
25-pound dog:	8–12 ounces daily, or two meals of 4–6 ounces each

Sample Cancer-Starving Raw Diet

Morning Meal

Feed a variety of high-fat protein sources, alternating between or mixing together any of the following:

Muscle Meat: especially high-fat varieties like ground beef, lamb, pork, or goat

Canned Fish: mackerel, salmon, or sardines (packed in water, not oil) are good options (steer clear of tuna)

Eggs: These are a great addition and can be added to every meal, if desired

Dairy: whole-milk yogurt and cottage cheese

Organ meats: including liver and kidney in small amounts. Feed small amounts daily, rather than larger amounts periodically, to avoid gastric upsets

Heart: another very healthy addition

Vegetables: to make up the fiber content in a home-cooked diet, offer a variety of the recommended vegetables listed in Figure 19.1, cooked and pureed

Evening Meal

Feed a variety of RMBs in the evening, such as:

Chicken necks, wings, backs, and frames,

Turkey necks

Beef necks and ribs

Pork necks, breast, feet, and tails

Lamb ribs

Cooked Diets

In order to feed your dog the most nutritious meals possible, cook the meat lightly. If your dog is a bit picky, use butter to add flavor and palatability (choose unsalted butter if your dog suffers from kidney or heart problems).

Each sample diet below is one meal for a 50-pound dog. The meat can be either cooked or fed raw. If cooking, mix the eggs and vegetables first, and then, when cooled, add the dairy. Remember, these diets are only guidelines. You can mix and match the meat, vegetables, eggs, or dairy to suit your dog's tastes.

Remember, feed these approximate amounts daily:

100-pound dog	2-3 pounds daily, or two meals of 1-1.5 pounds each
75-pound dog:	1.5-2 pounds daily, or two meals of 12-18 ounces each
50-pound dog:	1-1.5 pounds daily, or two meals of 8-12 ounces each
25-pound dog:	8-12 ounces daily, or two meals of 4-6 ounces each

Sample Cancer-Starving Home-Cooked Diets

Below are some sample cancer-starving home-cooked diets. Each of these recipes makes two meals for a fifty-pound dog, for one day's worth of feeding.

SAMPLE DIET ONE

12 ounces (1½ cups) ground beef

4 ounces (½ cup) beef liver or kidney, cooked in a small amount of butter

1 egg, scrambled or soft boiled

4 ounces (½ cup) steamed or cooked broccoli

2 ounces (¼ cup) whole-milk yogurt

Mix the meat, liver or kidney, egg, and broccoli well. Cool. Stir in the yogurt and serve.

SAMPLE DIET TWO

12 ounces (1½ cups) ground chicken

4 ounces (½ cup) chicken liver, cooked with a small amount of butter

1 egg, scrambled or soft boiled

4 ounces (½ cup) cooked cabbage

2 ounces (¼ cup) cottage cheese

Mix the meat, liver, egg, and cabbage well. When cool, stir in the cottage cheese and serve.

SAMPLE DIET THREE

12 ounces (1½ cup) ground pork

4 ounces (½ cup) pork or beef liver, cooked with a small amount of butter

1 egg, scrambled or soft boiled

4 ounces (½ cup) cooked zucchini

2 ounces (¼ cup) whole-milk yogurt

Mix the meat, liver, egg, and zucchini well. When cool, stir in the yogurt and serve.

SAMPLE DIET FOUR

12 ounces (1½ cup) canned mackerel or salmon

2 eggs, scrambled or soft boiled

4 ounces (½ cup) cooked kale or other dark leafy green

4 ounces (½ cup) cottage cheese

Mix the fish, egg, and kale well. When cool, stir in the yogurt and serve.

SUPPLEMENTS

To each meal, add:

900 milligrams calcium or 1 teaspoon ground eggshell (don't add this to meal four, which already gets enough calcium from the canned fish)

½ teaspoon green food blend that contains kelp, alfalfa, dulce, and spirulina

500 milligrams vitamin C per 25 pounds of body weight

100 IU vitamin E daily per 10 pounds of body weight

1,000 milligrams EPA fish or salmon oil daily per ten pounds of
body weight

Keep cans of mackerel, salmon, or sardines in the cupboard and a supply of frozen vegetables in your freezer. These will tide you over on those occasions when you run out of the food you usually use to make your homemade meals. Mackerel and vegetables make up a great quick meal; scrambled eggs with yogurt is another healthy and quick meal that you can make in a pinch.

Snacks

Sometimes you'll want to provide some snacks for your recuperating dog in between meals. Make sure the snacks you give are carbohydrate-free and high in protein and fat. Some easy treats include:

- Cheese cubes
- Hard-boiled eggs
- Beef jerky
- Liver squares

To make liver squares

Boil liver for ten to fifteen minutes. Drain well. Bake in a 250-degree oven for ten minutes per side. Let cool and cut into squares or cubes.

Food for Traveling

There are a few canned commercial foods that can be used for a dog with cancer if you're traveling and for one reason or another can't offer the usual homemade diet. These include:

- Wysong offers beef, chicken, duck, rabbit, and turkey with meat and organ "Au Jus Diets" (www.wysong.net/canned-wet-dog-food.php).
- Natures Variety offers a grain-free canned food in beef, chicken, and lamb flavors (http://naturesvariety.com/canine/pbeef/).
- Merrick Pet Foods offers several varieties that do not contain grains (www.merrickpetcare.com/store/canned_dog_food.php).
- Solid Gold Green Cow Tripe Canned Dog Food is another good choice (www.solidgoldhealth.com/products/showproduct.php?id=60&code=262).
- Evangers carries a variety of high quality canned meats like beef, chicken, rabbit, venison, and turkey.
- Hills Science Diet has developed a canned option called "N/D" that is suitable for dogs with cancer.

Supplements

SUPPLEMENTS FOR SMALL DOGS (TWENTY TO THIRTY-FIVE POUNDS). FOR TOY BREEDS, GIVE HALF THE SMALL DOG DOSE.

- Vitamin A: 1,000 milligrams twice a day
- Vitamin C: 500 milligrams twice a day
- Vitamin E: 50 IUs twice a day
- Vitamin B complex: 25 milligrams once a day
- Selenium: 10 micrograms once a day
- Bromelain: 50 milligrams twice a day
- Digestive enzymes with pancreatin: ¼ human dose per meal
- L-Glutamine: 100 milligrams twice a day
- Arginine: 50 milligrams twice a day
- EPA Fish Oil: 1,000 milligrams daily per ten to twenty pounds of body weight

SUPPLEMENTS FOR MEDIUM DOGS (THIRTY-FIVE TO SIXTY POUNDS)

- Vitamin A: 2,500 milligrams twice a day
- Vitamin C: 1,000 milligrams twice a day
- Vitamin E: 200 IUs twice a day
- Vitamin B complex: 50 milligrams once a day
- Selenium: 25 micrograms once a day
- Bromelain: 100 milligrams twice a day
- Digestive enzymes with pancreatin: ½ human dose per meal
- L-Glutamine: 300 milligrams twice a day
- Arginine: 100 milligrams once a day
- EPA Fish Oil: 1,000 milligrams daily per ten to twenty pounds of body weight

SUPPLEMENTS FOR LARGE DOGS (SIXTY TO NINETY POUNDS)

- Vitamin A: 5,000 milligrams twice a day
- Vitamin C: 2,000 milligrams twice a day
- Vitamin E: 400 IUs twice a day
- Vitamin B complex: 100 milligrams once a day
- Selenium: 50 micrograms once a day
- Bromelain: 200 milligrams twice a day
- Digestive enzymes with pancreatin: full human dose per meal
- L-Glutamine: 400 milligrams twice a day
- Arginine: 200 milligrams twice a day
- EPA Fish Oil: 1,000 milligrams daily per ten to twenty pounds of body weight

Berte's Immune Blend, from the B-Naturals company, carries a combination of the supplements above in a powdered blend for ease of dosage.

Chapter Twenty-One

Diets for Kidney Needs

The issue of nutrition for dogs with kidney problems has long been a topic of debate and confusion in the dog world. A number of persistent myths remain about what type of nutrition dogs with renal failure require. This makes it hard for dog owners to know what steps they need to take to offer their dogs the best care. When researching on the Internet, you're likely to find conflicting advice on the simplest of nutritional issues—from how much protein dogs with kidney problems need to what type of diet suits them best.

In this section we'll simplify this topic. Using some of the most current research, we'll look at the various causes of kidney problems and then discuss how you can offer your dog, whatever is the root of his or her kidney problems, the best nutrition for health and quality of life. While this chapter looks at symptoms and types of renal issues, the focus is on diet. Always work closely with your veterinarian to monitor your dog's condition and to gain information on medications and available treatments.

Symptoms

While veterinarians are the only people who can make a definite diagnosis, there are several telltale signs of kidney disease that you may notice at home, including:

- Weight loss
- Increased water consumption
- More frequent urination
- Vomiting and diarrhea
- Anemia (look for light-colored gums)
- Lethargy

Diagnosis

If you notice any of these symptoms, take your dog to the vet immediately for a check-up. A series of tests will determine if your dog does, indeed, have a kidney problem and, if so, the cause, extent, and type of kidney disease. These tests include blood work and urinalysis. If there is a problem, tests may show:

- A high BUN (Blood Urea Nitrogen)
- High levels of creatinine, phosphorus, and protein
- Low red blood count
- High enzyme counts, specifically amylase and lipase
- Decreased levels of sodium and HCO3
- Low specific gravity in the urinalysis

Keep an eye on the BUN, creatinine and phosphorus levels, as these specific blood levels can help you decide what dietary changes are needed.

Continued veterinarian care and guidance is a must with a renal diagnosis. Further problems may occur, such as anemia, pancreatitis, and nausea. Diet can help in many ways, but continued blood monitoring and urinalysis testing by your veterinarian are necessary.

Types of Kidney Problems

There are a number of types of kidney disease, many of which share symptoms, making a clear diagnosis difficult at times. A few of the more common types are:

Figure 21.1. Some Types of Kidney Problems.
Glomerulonephritis (protein-losing nephropathy)
Inherited or congenital kidney problems

Figure 21.1. Some Types of Kidney Problems. (continued)
Urinary tract infections
Diabetes insipidus
Fungal infections
Blockage of urine flow due to stones
Medications
Renal cancer
Systemic lupus erythematosis

Having a diagnosis and knowing what is causing it will help to determine if the problem is acute or chronic. A proper diagnosis is also important in order to rule out other problems that can affect kidney function such as adrenal disorders and bacterial infections. Some tests that may offer clues to finding a cause when renal problems occur are:

- Tick-Borne Disease Blood Panel
- Leptospirosis Blood Titer Panel
- ACTH Stim Test (to check for Cushing's or Addison's diseases)
- Urine Culture and Sensitivity Test (the best way to determine if bacteria are present in the urine, which, if undetected, can cause elevated BUN and creatinine blood levels)

Acute kidney problems are short-term issues that can often be treated. With the right diagnosis, medical care, and nutrition, a dog with acute renal problems that are detected early can often be returned to good health.

Chronic kidney problems, on the other hand, are not usually reversible, but can often be managed with the right care.

Diet

In order to feed a dog with kidney problems the best diet, it is important to be aware of your dog's current blood work numbers. Different stages and types of kidney problems require different diets, so keeping on top of this condition will help you know what nutritional changes or medications are necessary. My Rottweiler "Bean," for example, got sick in 2002. When his test results showed high BUN, creatinine, and phosphorus, I fed him a diet low in phosphorous. When his blood levels returned to normal, I was able to put him on a regular diet, but I continued to monitor his blood work, and how he felt, and was ready to make changes if needed. Once his renal values went up permanently, he remained on a low-phosphorus diet, along with subcutaneous fluids. His continued care was monitored closely, both by me and by our veterinarian.

Phosphorous and Sodium

One of the first things you should do if your dog's blood work indicates kidney problems is to evaluate whether or not the level of phosphorous in his or her diet needs to be reduced. (See "Further Reading" at the end of this chapter for a great list of low-phosphorous foods.) When Bean's creatinine level went higher than two, and his BUN was greater than eighty, I restricted both the phosphorus and sodium in his diet to ease the stress on his kidneys. This can be as simple as substituting dark chicken meat for white chicken meat and omitting high phosphorus foods like RMBs and canned fish.

Fortunately, most home-cooked and raw diets are already low in sodium, so not much change will be required. Steer clear of excessively salty foods, and be careful of commercial dog foods, which often rely on sodium as a preservative.

Protein

Research has shown that high-protein diets don't cause renal problems, and continuing dogs on good protein is important in renal disorders.[7] Aside from dogs suffering from end-stage chronic renal failure, who often require a reduced-phosphorus diet, dogs with renal problems still need a high level of quality proteins in their diets. Still, because of a few outdated assumptions that continue to hold influence in some canine circles, many veterinarians suggest lowering protein at any sign of renal problems. Such advice can do more harm than good—lowering the level of protein in a dog's diet puts them at risk of protein malnutrition, which can cause its own set of additional problems. Be sure to discuss this issue with your veterinarian if he or she suggests a reduced-protein diet for your dog.

Fat

Fat offers calories for energy and weight gain. More fat in the meat means less protein, and therefore less phosphorous. So keep up the fat, but be aware that dogs with renal conditions are more prone to pancreatitis. Keep an eye on the amylase and lipase levels in your dog's blood work, as they can indicate the first signs of pancreatitis. Always discuss any symptoms of gastric upset with your veterinarian as soon as they occur.

Carbohydrates

Certain grains tend to be high in phosphorous and are best avoided. All grains should be cooked thoroughly. While I have listed plain Malt-O-Meal and sushi rice as selections in the recipes below, Figure 21.2 is a chart of several foods, along with their phosphorous contents, that can be mixed and matched within these recipes for added variety.

Figure 21.2. Phosphorous Contents of Various Low-Phosphorous Foods.	
Per Cup	Phosphorus Content
Tapioca, Pearl	10.6 milligrams
Rice, white, glutinous, cooked	14 milligrams
Rice noodles, cooked	35.2 milligrams
Couscous, cooked	35 milligrams
Cream of Rice cereal, plain, cooked	41 milligrams
Cream of Wheat cereal, plain, cooked	43 milligrams
Malt-O-Meal, plain, cooked	67 milligrams
Potato, white, cooked	68 milligrams
Sweet potato, cooked	105 milligrams
Source: www.nutritiondata.com	

Some of these are more palatable than others and your dog may have favorites. Try as many as possible for variety. Cook any of these with butter, and add a few tablespoons of heavy cream for additional flavor and calories. The website www.nutritiondata.com is a wonderful tool for determining phosphorus and fat content in your dog's diet.

Remember, feed these approximate amounts daily:

100-pound dog:	2–3 pounds daily, or two meals of 1–1.5 pounds each
75-pound dog:	1.5–2 pounds daily, or two meals of 12–18 ounces each
50-pound dog:	1–1.5 pounds daily, or two meals of 8–12 ounces each
25-pound dog:	8–12 ounces daily, or two meals of 4–6 ounces each

Dogs with renal issues may do better on several small meals a day. As always, offer plenty of variety.

Sample Diets for Dogs with Kidney Problems

Dogs suffering severe kidney problems often experience loss of appetite, so switching food often and creativity in the diet is essential. With this in mind, let's take a look at a few sample diets, designed for a fifty-pound dog. Each recipe is for one day; divide into two or three portions as desired.

SAMPLE DIET ONE

  11 ounces (approximately 1⅓ cups) cooked sticky rice (sushi rice)

  2 teaspoons unsalted butter

  11 ounces (approximately 1⅓ cups) high-fat ground beef

  2 cooked egg whites (no yolk)

  1 teaspoon ground eggshell

Mix the rice, butter, and ground beef. Add the egg whites and ground eggshell. Mix well and serve.

SAMPLE DIET TWO

  12 ounces (1½ cups) cooked unflavored Malt-O-Meal

  1½ tablespoons unsalted butter

  8 ounces (1 cup) cooked dark meat chicken

  1 egg

  2 tablespoons heavy cream

  Grated cheese, such as parmesan, ricotta, or cheddar (optional)

Mix together Malt-O-Meal and butter and set mixture aside to cool. Add chicken, egg, cream, and cheese (if using). Mix well and serve.

SAMPLE DIET THREE

  8 ounces (1 cup) cooked sticky rice

  2 teaspoons unsalted butter

  6 ounces (¾ cup) boiled sweet potatoes (substitute potatoes,
      if desired)

8 ounces (1 cup) ground pork or lamb

3 egg whites

1½ teaspoons ground eggshell

Stir together rice, butter, sweet potatoes, ground meat, egg whites, and eggshell. Mix well and serve.

OTHER RECOMMENDED FOODS

Green tripe is another good low-phosphorus choice that can be substituted for meat. Look for it at outlets that sell frozen raw diets for dogs. It is also available in cans.

Drained mackerel or salmon can be substituted for the meat for variety. (Remember not to add calcium if you're feeding fish with bones.) Because of the bone, fish is high in phosphorus and so should be used sparingly. Avoid tuna, which is high in mercury.

Because of their high fat content, pork and lamb are great choices for dogs with kidney issues. Do monitor for symptoms of pancreatitis, as dogs with renal issues frequently develop this condition, which requires a reduced-fat diet. (For information on the symptoms of pancreatitis, see "Chapter Twenty-Two: Diets for Liver Needs.")

Beef kidney, liver, and egg yolks, in small amounts, are also good additions to the diet. While these are high in phosphorus, they also provide nutrients your dog needs.

Supplements

Try the following supplements to support and protect your dog's kidneys:

FISH OR SALMON OIL

Omega-3 fish and salmon oils have been proven to protect the kidneys. For best results, offer 1,000 milligrams per ten pounds of body weight daily

COQ10

Recent studies show that COQ10 helps reduce creatinine levels and restore normal kidney function. Offer two milligrams per pound of body weight.

VITAMINS A, B, AND E

These are great for supporting the kidneys and should be given regularly.

Further Reading

There is a wonderful Yahoo! Group called K9KidneyDiet (http:// groups.yahoo.com/group/K9KidneyDiet/), whose extremely helpful members can answer many questions you might have. There you'll also find diets and a wealth of kidney-related information.

A more detailed account of how to care for a dog with renal failure can be found at Mary Straus' website, (www.dogaware.com/ kidney.html), where you'll also find a wealth of information on how to feed and treat dogs with kidney problems and an excellent list of low-phosphorous foods.

Chapter Twenty-Two

Diets for Liver Needs

The liver is an amazing organ, responsible for a variety of complex jobs within the body. Synthesizing proteins, metabolizing fats, and filtering the blood are among the liver's functions. Precisely because the liver works so hard and does so much, there are a lot of things that can go wrong. All kinds of stresses and strains on the body—from certain drugs, injuries, gastric upsets, and illness—can affect liver function, and with it, your dog's quality of life.

Diagnosis

Liver problems are quite common among canines, so it's important to know how to recognize and treat any liver issues before they become too serious.

Symptoms

Liver problems can cause a wide variety of symptoms, such as:

- Weight loss and debilitation
- Loss of energy and interest in normal activities
- Diarrhea and upset stomach
- Intermittent vomiting and constipation
- Light tan or grey stools
- Darker, sometimes orange urine
- Fluid retention in the stomach
- Jaundice
- Aberrant behaviors like pacing, circling, or even seizures
- Excess water drinking and urination[8]

Causes of Liver Disease

The liver is in charge of cleaning the blood and metabolizing drugs, two jobs that can put it into contact with a lot of toxic substances, some of which can cause disease. Indeed, its many functions mean it can be affected by a whole range of problems, including:

- Viral or bacterial diseases
- Fungal infections
- Toxic poisoning
- Altered blood flow disorders
- Copper storage disease
- Cancer
- Injury or trauma
- Pancreatitis
- Chronic gastric upsets

The liver is a tough organ. It keeps on running even when it's heavily diseased, making early diagnosis difficult at times. Although noticeable symptoms can and do show themselves, they often don't appear until the problem has been present for some time. So keep an eye out for the symptoms, and always check with your veterinarian if you see changes in your dog's health.

A veterinarian will usually perform a blood panel check-up to assess the health of the liver, and to determine what treatment, if any, is needed. Further tests like radiographs, ultrasounds, biopsies, and bile acid tests may be performed, depending on the severity of the symptoms.

Treatment

There are a wide array of ways to treat liver problems, some of which you can take charge of at home. In the more severe cases, your dog may require surgery, IV therapy, or diuretics. In many cases, however, you can help start the healing process by taking very simple steps at home.

If your dog has suffered liver damage as a result of exposure to a poison or medication, the best thing to do is simply remove that substance from your dog's system, allowing the liver to heal and regenerate. This can be as simple as removing the medication, or putting a stop to possible behavioral causes like garbage scavenging, for example.

Always check the medications your dog is taking carefully; read all the inserts and talk to your veterinarian about any side effects. While medications are a common cause of toxic poisoning, contaminated water, poisons, and even pollutants found in the soil (think herbicides and pesticides) can all contribute to liver problems, too, so be aware of possible triggers in your environment.[9]

Though the liver can regenerate itself, it still needs a helping hand. A varied homemade diet and regular supplements can go a long way to reversing liver problems, no matter how severe. The same holds true for prevention—a considered homemade diet is the best defense against liver problems occurring in the first place.

Diet

Much of the confusion surrounding nutrition for canines with liver problems has had to do with diet—which foods suit them best? How much fat can they handle? The good news is the best diet for a dog with liver problems is a fresh, homemade one. If you've been feeding a raw or home cooked diet and supplementing well, you shouldn't have to make too many changes.

Protein

The common wisdom for dogs with liver problems is to restrict protein, which isn't always necessary. It isn't the protein that does the damage to a dog with liver problems, but the ammonia contained in certain animal proteins. Furthermore, this ammonia is only problematic for certain liver ailments, such as certain shunt disorders or end-stage liver disease. Know what type of liver disease your dog has to determine the best diet. High-quality protein is crucial for organ health, regeneration, and repair; giving too little can restrict recovery. For best results, offer your dog high-quality proteins. If your dog has a condition that compromises his or her ability to process ammonia, then opt for low-ammonia proteins.

Figure 22.1. Good Protein Sources for Dogs with Liver Problems.
Low-Ammonia Protein Sources
Eggs
Low-fat cottage cheese
Yogurt
Chicken (with skin and visible fat removed)
Fish

Although red meat and organs are higher in ammonia, don't eliminate them entirely—they contain several nutrients that will help with your dog's liver function. If your dog's condition improves (assuming this isn't a shunt disorder or other condition that can't be repaired), you can begin adding more red meat.

Carbohydrates

Many diets designed for dogs with liver diseases lower the protein and add carbohydrates to compensate. The ability of dogs with liver problems to process large amounts of carbohydrates can decrease markedly if they are prone to digestive upsets and lack of appetite. Though some carbohydrates are needed, don't rely on them too heavily. The best sources are complex carbohydrates, which offer soluble fiber to help absorb ammonia and toxins. Insoluble fiber sources are also helpful, so offer a good mix of the two.

Figure 22.2. Good Sources of Soluble and Insoluble Fiber for Dogs with Liver Disease.	
Insoluble Fiber Sources	Soluble Fiber Sources
Oatmeal	Vegetables
Bran muffins	Oatmeal
Whole-grain pasta	Barley
Whole-wheat bread	Rye
Pulped vegetable skins and rinds	Beans
Ground psyllium husks	Carrots
Canned plain pumpkin	Green beans

Fat

Dogs always need high quality fats for energy and calorie production. Dogs with liver disease are no different, but you need to be careful not to put too much stress on the liver by offering excessive fat or fats of poor quality. Offer moderate amounts of the most easily digestible fats, removing the extra fat from the meats you serve and offering low-fat dairy. It may be advisable to serve several small meals daily. Instead of two good-sized meals, try serving four to six smaller meals.

Figure 22.3. Good Fat Sources for Dogs with Liver Problems.
Fat Sources
Meat fat
Omega-3 fatty acids like fish body oil or salmon oil

Remember, feed these approximate amounts daily:

100-pound dog:	2–3 pounds daily, or two meals of 1–1.5 pounds each
75-pound dog:	1.5–2 pounds daily, or two meals of 12–18 ounces each
50-pound dog:	1–1.5 pounds daily, or two meals of 8–12 ounces each
25-pound dog:	8–12 ounces daily, or two meals of 4–6 ounces each

Sample Diets for Dogs with Liver Problems

Here are sample diets for a fifty-pound dog with liver problems. Each diet is for one day; divide the recipe into several smaller meals.

SAMPLE DIET ONE

6 ounces (¾ cup) low-fat cottage cheese

6 ounces (¾ cup) cooked chicken

1 egg

6 ounces (¾ cup) cooked oatmeal

4 ounces (½ cup) canned pumpkin

Combine cottage cheese, chicken, egg, oatmeal and pumpkin. Mix well and serve.

SAMPLE DIET TWO

6 ounces (¾ cup) cooked cod

1 egg

6 ounces (¾ cup) cooked oatmeal

6 ounces (¾ cup) cooked broccoli, cauliflower, or sweet potato

4 ounces (½ cup) low-fat yogurt

Combine cooked cod, oatmeal, and mashed vegetables. When cool, stir in the yogurt. Mix well and serve.

SAMPLE DIET THREE

> 6 ounces (¾ cup) drained and rinsed canned or cooked salmon
>
> 3 eggs, scrambled
>
> 4 ounces (½ cup) low-fat cottage cheese
>
> 6 ounces (¾ cup) cooked barley
>
> 2 slices whole-wheat bread

> Combine the fish, eggs, cottage cheese, barley, and bread. Mix well and serve.

You'll notice that diets one and two will need some added calcium. Add half a teaspoon of ground eggshell (or 900 milligrams of calcium carbonate or calcium citrate) for every pound of food served. During convalescence, you needn't worry about balancing the diet for a few weeks if they will be returning to their normal diets.

Low-salt diets can help prevent the fluid retention common in some forms of liver disease, so try not to add extra salt to the diet. Be sure to drain and rinse canned fish thoroughly. Fortunately, home-cooked diets are naturally low in salt.

Supplements

Much of what your dog will need to get back on track will be offered in the diet, but to give your dog the best chance at recovery and a long healthy life, use a combination of the following supplements:

PROBIOTIC POWDER

Dogs with liver disease need help producing vitamin K, making this blend a great addition to their diet. It also offers the beneficial bacteria needed to keep the good flora and fauna that may be lost due to diarrhea, vomiting, and stress.

GREEN FOODS

Kelp, dulce, alfalfa, and kelp contain trace minerals that are perfect for a dog suffering from liver disease.

VITAMINS B, C, AND E

Dogs with liver disease often have trouble retaining enough water-soluble vitamins such as vitamin C and the B vitamins. Give vitamin C at about 500 milligrams per twenty-five pounds of body weight daily and fifty milligrams of B-complex per fifty pounds of body weight daily.

SALMON OR FISH OIL

Omega-3 fatty acids, as always, are very helpful. Give 1,000 mg per twenty to thirty pounds of body weight daily.

DIGESTIVE ENZYMES

Since liver disease can compromise the body's capacity to break down fats, a good digestive enzyme is recommended. Use one that contains the enzymes pancreatin and pancrealipase from animal sources.

MILK THISTLE

This herb, available in either capsules or liquid tincture, has been found to help regenerate the liver and remove toxins.

SAM-E

Several studies have shown SAM-e (also known as *denosyl*) is an excellent booster of liver function. Give 200 milligrams per fifty pounds of body weight in between meals.

L-CARNITINE

This amino acid is often found lacking in human patients with advanced cirrhosis of the liver, and studies have shown it to be a good supplement for canine liver support. Give approximately 500 milligrams daily per fifty pounds of body weight.

L-ARGININE

Another liver-supporting amino acid, give about 250 milligrams daily per fifty pounds of body weight.

Chapter Twenty-Three

Diet and Pancreatitis

Dogs use their pancreas to release the enzymes they need to digest food when it reaches the small intestine. Pancreatitis is a condition in which the pancreas is inflamed. This condition can cause the release of too many enzymes within the pancreas itself, which can lead to further inflammation and, in more severe cases, consumption of its own tissue leading to severe pain and discomfort. In this chapter we'll learn at how to help prevent pancreatitis, as well as how to care for and feed dogs once this does occur.

Diagnosis

A common canine ailment, pancreatitis shares a number of symptoms with other conditions, which can make it difficult to diagnose accurately.

Symptoms

Signs your dog might be suffering from pancreatitis include:

- Loss of appetite
- Vomiting
- Arching of the back, indicating stomach pain
- Diarrhea

If you suspect from that your dog might be affected with pancreatitis, get him or her to the veterinarian as soon as possible.

Causes of Pancreatitis

Common wisdom has long held that fat was the primary cause of pancreatitis, but that isn't actually the case. High-fat diets can aggravate a diseased pancreas, but fat itself doesn't usually cause the condition. While there is still some degree of uncertainty about the exact cause of pancreatitis, the most recent research suggests the following factors contribute to the condition:

- Genetic conditions such as hyperlipidemia (high cholesterol and/or triglycerides), often found in Miniature Schnauzers, Briards, and Shetland Sheepdogs
- Hypercalcemia, caused by parathyroid conditions or over supplementing with calcium
- Certain drugs, including some steroids (such as prednisone), tetracyclines and other sulfonamide antibiotics, metronidazole (flagyl), azothiaprin (imuran), estrogen, long acting antacids (cimetidine/Tagament, ranitidine/Zantac), diuretics, acetaminophen (Tylenol), and some chemotherapy drugs including l-asparaginase
- Thyroid problems
- Obesity
- Exposure to common insecticides including organophosphates
- Cushing's disease (hyperadrenocorticism), hypothyroidism, liver disease, and diabetes
- While it has been indicated that disc disease or spinal cord injuries may cause pancreatitis, it may be more likely that steroids are the real cause, as these drugs are commonly used to treat such injuries

Types of Pancreatitis

Pancreatitis, as with kidney problems, comes in two forms: acute and chronic.

Acute pancreatitis is usually restricted to one incident with a discernible cause, like a reaction to a drug or an illness. Most acute pancreatic incidents only happen once.

Chronic pancreatitis is when several acute occurrences happen over time, damaging the pancreas. The pancreas can also suffer long-term damage from diseases and conditions like hypothyroidism.

Treatment

If your dog's condition is severe enough to warrant immediate treatment, he or she may be hospitalized for several days to undergo intravenous fluid therapy. While in the hospital, the dog will usually be fasted from food and water for several days while the pain is treated.

What can you do at home? Aside from diet and supplementation, be sure to always offer your dog a lot of daily physical exercise, which will keep him or her lean and healthy and help to prevent attacks.

Diet

There are a few straightforward steps to take in the diet of a dog affected by pancreatitis. The first is to reduce fat. While not a cause of pancreatitis, fat tends to over stimulate the pancreas while it's trying to recover. Lowering the amount of fat in the diet makes it easier for your dog to convalesce.

The pancreas is in charge of producing insulin to control blood glucose levels. It's not surprising to learn that pancreatitis and diabetes are closely linked. Dogs with diabetes are often prone to pancreatitis and vice versa. If you suspect a problem with your dog's insulin levels it's a good idea to watch the amount of sugar in his or her diet, limiting high-glycemic vegetables, fruits, and honey. Smaller, more frequent meals also help stabilize your dog's glucose levels while keeping enzyme activity at normal, healthy levels.

For chronic cases, check with your veterinarian about ongoing care. Some dogs might need enzymes temporarily added to their diet to help get their digestion back on track, while others may need them permanently.

Recommended Foods

Dogs suffering pancreatitis do well on low-glycemic vegetables and some starchier foods, which give them some of the calories lost when dietary fat is reduced. Remember to cook the vegetables well, and make sure the grains are well cooked to make them easier to digest.

Figure 23.1. Recommended Dietary Make-up for Dogs with Pancreatitis.

Low-Fat Animal Proteins (50%)	Low-Glycemic Vegetables (25%)	Starchy Foods (25%)
White meat chicken (with skin and excess fat removed)	Broccoli or cauliflower	Sweet potatoes
Lean or low-fat ground beef (if cooked, drain excess fat, or boil to remove most of the fat.)	Cabbage	White potatoes
	Summer squashes (zucchini, yellow crookneck squash, etc.)	Oatmeal
Beef heart or roast, with excess fat removed	Dark leafy greens	Rice
Beef kidney and liver (small amounts)	Romaine lettuce	Barley
Egg whites	Collard greens	
Low-fat or nonfat plain yogurt or cottage cheese	Mustard greens	
	Spinach	

Sample Diets for Dogs with Pancreatitis

The sample diets below should only normally be needed for a few days or weeks during the recovery period after a pancreatic attack. If your dog is prone to chronic pancreatitis, he or she may need to be kept on a diet of small, low-fat meals like these for life.

If you are feeding these meals over a long period of time, calcium will need to be added (give 900 milligrams per pound of food served). If you are just using these diets in the short-term (less than two weeks), adding calcium isn't necessary.

With the proper care, dogs suffering from pancreatitis can often return to full health. When they do, you can gradually return them to their normal diet. Please feed a dog recovering from pancreatitis frequent, small meals. Dividing these recipes into four meals per day is helpful to ease the load on the pancreas during recovery.

Remember, feed these approximate amounts daily:

100-pound dog:	2–3 pounds daily, or two meals of 1–1.5 pounds each
75-pound dog:	1.5–2 pounds daily, or two meals of 12–18 ounces each
50-pound dog:	1–1.5 pounds daily, or two meals of 8–12 ounces each
25-pound dog:	8–12 ounces daily, or two meals of 4–6 ounces each

Each of these recipes is for a day's worth of meals for a fifty-pound adult dog with pancreatitis. Please divide each recipe into two to four smaller meals during the day, for ease of digestion.

SAMPLE DIET ONE

12 ounces (1½ cups) cooked beef heart chunks, fat drained

2 ounces (¼ cup) cooked spinach

4 ounces (½ cup) cooked broccoli

6 ounces (¾ cup) cooked sweet potato

Digestive enzymes, probiotics, and l-glutamine (500 milligrams daily per 20 pounds of body weight)

Combine the cooked meat and vegetables. When cool, add the supplements. Mix well and serve.

SAMPLE DIET TWO

8 ounces (1 cup) cooked chicken breast

2 ounces (¼ cup) cooked cabbage

4 ounces (½ cup) cooked zucchini

6 ounces (¾ cup) cup white potato

4 ounces (½ cup) low-fat or nonfat plain yogurt

Digestive enzymes, probiotics, and l-glutamine (500 milligrams daily per 20 pounds of body weight)

Combine the cooked chicken and vegetables. When cool, add the yogurt and supplements. Mix well and serve.

SAMPLE DIET THREE

8 ounces (1 cup) boiled lean ground beef, fat drained

4 ounces (½ cup) cooked beef kidney, fat trimmed

2 ounces (¼ cup) cooked kale

4 ounces (½ cup) yellow crookneck squash

6 ounces (¾ cup) oatmeal

Digestive enzymes, probiotics, and l-glutamine (500 milligrams daily per 20 pounds of body weight)

Combine the cooked beef kidney, vegetables, and oatmeal. When cool, add the supplements. Mix well and serve.

SAMPLE DIET FOUR

8 ounces (1 cup) cooked stew beef or cut up lean roast, fat drained

4 ounces (½ cup) cup cooked broccoli

2 ounces (¼ cup) cooked zucchini

6 ounces (¾ cup) cooked barley

4 ounces (½ cup) cup low-fat or nonfat cottage cheese

Digestive enzymes, probiotics, and l-glutamine (500 milligrams daily per 20 pounds of body weight)

Combine the cooked beef, vegetables, and barley. When cool, add the cottage cheese and supplements. Mix well and serve.

DON'T FORGET

Feed the meals in three or four portions daily, and add digestive supplements with every meal. You may cook the meat or feed raw, as you prefer. If cooking, add the fully cooked vegetables and dairy to the meat as it cools.

Supplements

Supplements are important for dogs with pancreatitis, as they need all the help they can get to get their digestive balance back. Try offering:

DIGESTIVE ENZYMES, PROBIOTICS, AND L-GLUTAMINE

Digestive enzymes help pre-digest fat in the stomach, which eases the load for the pancreas and liver. Probiotics (beneficial bacteria) help restore the friendly bacteria to the digestive tract. L-glutamine helps heal the digestive tract. Give 500 milligrams of l-glutamine daily per twenty pounds of body weight.

EPA FISH OIL

A must in every diet, fish oil helps reduce inflammation. Give 1,000 milligrams daily per twenty pounds of body weight.

VITAMINS C, E, AND B COMPLEX

As your dog improves, you can add vitamins C and E and a B complex. A fifty-pound dog should get about 500 milligrams of vitamin C, 400 IU of vitamin E and a B50 complex each day.

Chapter Twenty-Four

Low-Glycemic Diets

In this section we are going to look at how the sugar in carbohydrates can affect epilepsy, hypothyroidism, diabetes, allergies, arthritis, and yeast infections, and how a low-glycemic diet is a good defense against all of these conditions.

The best diets for dogs are high in protein and fat and low in carbohydrates. Dogs don't have a nutritional need for carbohydrates. In addition to adding more bulk to the stool and stressing the digestive system, the sugars in carbohydrates directly affect the blood sugar in the body. Canines are designed to make glucose from proteins, which keep the dog's blood sugar level stable. Meals high in grains or starches cause blood sugar to rise and then fall, which can lead to a range of health problems. Fluctuating blood sugar levels have been shown to:

- Directly affect diabetes
- Trigger epileptic seizures
- Aggravate arthritis
- Affect thyroid conditions
- Feed cancer cells

If your dog has been diagnosed with epilepsy, hypothyroidism, diabetes, allergies, arthritis, or yeast infections, help is at hand. There are several simple modifications you can make to the homemade diet to manage these conditions, or to prevent them if you feel your dog might be susceptible.

Let's take a look now at what foods and supplements are right for each condition and how you can manage and prevent these conditions through homemade diets. These conditions will be divided into two different diets: low-fat, low-glycemic diets, and regular-fat, low-glycemic diets.

Epilepsy

While the connection between grains and seizures is still being researched, a number of studies suggest that feeding carbohydrates can increase the risks of seizure activity, either by making blood sugar level fluctuations more extreme or by causing allergic reactions due to gluten intolerance.[10] The best defense is a fresh-food diet, with low to medium levels of fat, high levels of animal protein, and few carbohydrates.

Jake's Story

Picked up as a stray when he was six weeks old, Jake, a Doberman/ Labrador mix, began having seizures when he was three years old. Jake was what is called a "clusterer," meaning he always had multiple seizures close together. Despite trying everything from conventional medication to acupuncture, his owner, Jo, was unable to get the seizures under control. After exhausting all the usual medical avenues, Jo started to look elsewhere for alternative treatments, joining an online canine epilepsy group. One of the things recommended by the group was a raw diet. With nothing left to lose, Jo started Jake on a new raw diet.

Within five months Jake had gone from having seven seizures every two weeks to one a month. Her vet, she says, was "astonished" at the drastic improvement a raw, fresh food diet had made when all other treatments had failed.

SUPPLEMENTS

Fish oil, vitamin E, and digestive enzymes are all good supplements for dogs suffering from epilepsy. Additionally adding a quality B complex vitamin has been proven to fight seizures in both humans and animals. DMG, made from a derivative of glycine, has also shown promising results in slowing down or stopping seizure activity. For dogs, the liquid form given by dropper in the gum line appears to work best.

Diabetes

Diabetes is closely linked with obesity in humans and canines. Type I Diabetes is the type that is most common in dogs and can be supported and possibly prevented though diet. Offer a low-carbohydrate diet with moderate levels of fat and high levels of protein, which recent studies have suggested help balance sugar levels in the bloodstream.[11] If you do want to offer carbohydrates, make sure they're well cooked and low-glycemic.

Prevention is always the best cure, so try to feed an easily digestible, nutrient-rich fresh-food diet.

SUPPLEMENTS

Carnitine, chromium, and vitamin A are great supplements for dogs with diabetes, as are Fish Oil, B complex vitamins, vitamin E, and digestive enzymes, which help in the digestion of fats.

Hypothyroidism

Because the thyroid regulates so many of the body's functions, symptoms of an underactive thyroid (hypothyroidism), can range from weight gain to skin problems to pancreatitis. While the symptoms may be complicated, the treatment is pretty straightforward. A simple blood test at your veterinarian's office can be used to diagnose hypothyroidism. If your dog is found to have an underactive thyroid, your veterinarian can prescribe thyroid medications to help correct it.

Dogs with hypothyroidism tend to do better on medium-fat, low-glycemic homemade diets that offer a high level of protein. Steer clear of foods that suppress thyroid function, like cabbage, broccoli, turnips, rutabaga, mustard greens, kale, spinach, Brussels sprouts, peaches, pears, strawberries, cauliflower, potatoes, and corn. If you do offer these foods, be sure to cook them thoroughly, which helps to remove the goitrogens that suppress the thyroid function. Even then, they shouldn't make up more than a small part of the diet. Also avoid soy, which can block minerals such calcium, iodine, and magnesium that dogs with thyroid problems need for good health.

SUPPLEMENTS

Supplements for a dog with hypothyroidism should include fish oil, B complex vitamins, vitamin E, and digestive enzymes, which will help with fat digestion.

Low-Fat, Low-Glycemic Diets

Epilepsy, hypothyroidism, and diabetes all require lower fat diets. The meat in these diets can be served cooked or raw.

Remember, feed these approximate amounts daily:

100-pound dog:	2–3 pounds daily, or two meals of 1–1.5 pounds each
75-pound dog:	1.5–2 pounds daily, or two meals of 12–18 ounces each
50-pound dog:	1–1.5 pounds daily, or two meals of 8–12 ounces each
25-pound dog:	8–12 ounces daily, or two meals of 4–6 ounces each

The recipes below are for a fifty-pound adult dog for one day's serving. Please divide each recipe into two or more smaller meals per day.

SAMPLE DIET ONE

    6 ounces (¾ cup) low-fat ground beef
    2 ounces (¼ cup) beef liver or kidney
    2 egg whites, no yolks, scrambled or soft boiled
    4 ounces (½ cup) steamed or boiled broccoli
    4 ounces (½ cup) cooked yellow crookneck squash
    4 ounces nonfat yogurt

Serve meat cooked or raw, combined with the cooked vegetables, eggs, and yogurt. If serving the meat cooked, wait until it has cooled before stirring in the yogurt.

SAMPLE DIET TWO

    8 ounces (1 cup) white meat chicken, skin removed

    4 ounces (½ cup) chicken liver

    2 egg whites, no yolk, scrambled or soft boiled

    4 ounces (½ cup) steamed or boiled spinach

    4 ounces (½ cup) cooked cabbage

    4 ounces nonfat (½ cup) cottage cheese

Serve meat cooked or raw, combined with the cooked vegetables, eggs, and cottage cheese. If serving the meat cooked, wait until it has cooled before stirring in the cottage cheese.

SAMPLE DIET THREE

    8 ounces (1 cup) beef heart, cut into small pieces

    2 ounces (¼ cup) pork or beef liver

    2 egg whites, scrambled or soft boiled

    4 ounces (½ cup) steamed or boiled bok choy or Chinese cabbage

    4 ounces (½ cup) cooked zucchini

    4 ounces (½ cup) nonfat yogurt

Serve meat cooked or raw, combined with the cooked vegetables, eggs, and yogurt. If serving the meat cooked, wait until it has cooled before stirring in the yogurt.

SAMPLE DIET FOUR

    8 ounces (1 cup) mackerel or salmon, rinsed and drained

    2 egg whites, scrambled or soft boiled

    4 ounces (½ cup) cooked broccoli

    4 ounces (½ cup) cooked kale or other dark leafy green

    4 ounces (½ cup) nonfat cottage cheese

Cook vegetables and eggs (there is no need to cook the canned fish as it is already cooked) and combine, along with the cottage cheese. No calcium is needed because mackerel, salmon, or sardines already contain soft, steamed bones, which provide ample calcium.

SUPPLEMENTS

1,400 milligrams calcium, or ¾ teaspoon ground eggshell
1 teaspoon green food with kelp and spirulina
500 milligrams vitamin C daily per 25 pounds of body weight
100 IU vitamin E daily per 20 pounds of body weight
1,000 milligrams EPA fish or salmon oil daily per ten pounds of
    body weight

Arthritis

If your dog has arthritis, the main concern is to try to reduce the inflammation while keeping weight down. A dog with arthritis needs to stay lean to limit stress on the joints, so avoid grains and starches, which can be fattening. Stay away from starchy nightshade vegetables like tomatoes, potatoes, eggplants, and peppers, which can aggravate inflammation. If your dog is lean, follow the regular low-glycemic diets below. If your dog needs to lose some weight, follow the low-fat, low-glycemic diets above.

SUPPLEMENTS

EPA fish oil is a great help with inflammation. Formulas with glucosamine, chondroitin, and manganese can help lubricate the joints and bring down swelling. If you're looking for a natural option, liquid yucca herbal tincture helps fight inflammation. Give at one drop per ten pounds of body weight with meals. Be sure to give yucca with meals to avoid stomach upset. (For more information, see "Chapter Twenty-Six: Diet and Joint Problems.")

Allergies

With all the chemicals around these days, the exact cause of allergies can be difficult to pinpoint. If you suspect your dog has an allergy, there are two questions you should ask:

- Is this an allergy, or could these be symptoms of another health issue?
- If it is an allergy, it is an environmental allergy or food related allergy?

Age can be a good tool to help you discern the cause of an allergic reaction. Young dogs are more likely to suffer an environmental allergy than a food allergy.[12]

If you suspect your dog has reacted to something in the environment, make a quick survey of things you've recently introduced into the home—carpeting, bedding, household cleaners, or yard sprays are all common household allergy triggers—and bathe your dog frequently. Bathing will wash the offending allergens off the dog, at least temporarily. This should help rule environmental allergies either in or out.

Food allergies, on the other hand, are more difficult to identify and determine, especially if you're feeding commercial foods because they contain so many ingredients.

If you suspect a food allergy you might want to try an elimination diet. This means trying food that hasn't been fed before. This is done by introducing one new protein and one new carbohydrate for several weeks. Though elimination diets can be a good way to root out an allergy, return to offering a variety of foods as soon as you can. Sticking to a limited diet for too long only heightens the risk of developing an allergy to the new food.

With its fewer and fresher ingredients, home cooking is a simple way to offer better nutrition while lessening the risk of potential allergies. And you'll also have control over what your dog eats. The recipe suggestions in this chapter provide a solid foundation for a balanced diet, with the option of picking and choosing the ingredients that best suit your dog, area, and budget. Again, always offer your dog the best variety of good quality foods you can, as this provides the best defense against all health problems.

SUPPLEMENTS

If your dog has a skin reaction because of an allergy, fish oil can really help reduce coat and skin inflammation.

Yeast

Yeast problems can have a number of causes. Dogs with allergies often itch and scratch their way to yeast infections, while common medications used to treat skin problems—steroids and antibiotics are two examples—can also encourage yeast growth.

The symptoms arising from yeast infections are often very similar to those of allergic reactions. Without proper diagnosis and treatment, yeast problems and allergies can go back and forth, causing your dog a lot of discomfort. As always, make a trip to your veterinarian if you think your dog has a yeast problem. The veterinarian will usually take a skin culture to look for both bacteria and yeast, which will help determine a course of treatment.

As far as diet is concerned, yeast thrives on sugar, so sticking to low-glycemic meals, like the sample diets in this chapter, will help. Frequent baths with an oatmeal-based shampoo followed by a rinse of white vinegar and water (mixed in a one-to-one ratio) will also help.

SUPPLEMENTS

Probiotics made from beneficial bacteria and olive leaf extract are great for fighting yeast overgrowth. These are given orally or combined with food.

Diet

Now let's take a look at some sample diets. The following low-glycemic, high-protein diets are designed for dogs with allergies, arthritis, and yeast problems.

The meat in the sample diets here can be cooked or served raw.

Low Glycemic, Regular Fat Diets

Remember, feed these approximate amounts daily:

100-pound dog:	2–3 pounds daily, or two meals of 1–1.5 pounds each
75-pound dog:	1.5–2 pounds daily, or two meals of 12–18 ounces each
50-pound dog:	1–1.5 pounds daily, or two meals of 8–12 ounces each
25-pound dog:	8–12 ounces daily, or two meals of 4–6 ounces each

Here are sample low-glycemic diets for a fifty-pound dog for one day's serving. Please divide each recipe into two or more smaller meals per day.

SAMPLE DIET ONE

8 ounces (1 cup) regular fat ground beef

2 ounces (¼ cup) beef liver or kidney

2 eggs, scrambled or soft boiled

4 ounces (½ cup) steamed or boiled broccoli

4 ounces (½ cup) cooked yellow crookneck squash

4 ounces (½ cup) whole-milk yogurt

Serve meat cooked or raw, combined with the cooked vegetables, eggs, and yogurt. If serving the meat cooked, wait until it has cooled before stirring in the yogurt.

SAMPLE DIET TWO

    8 ounces (1 cup) ground chicken

    4 ounces (½ cup) chicken liver

    1 egg, scrambled or soft boiled

    4 ounces (½ cup) steamed or boiled spinach

    4 ounces (½ cup) cooked cabbage

    4 ounces (½ cup) whole-milk cottage cheese

Serve meat cooked or raw, combined with the cooked vegetables, eggs, and cottage cheese. If serving the meat cooked, wait until it has cooled before stirring in the cottage cheese.

SAMPLE DIET THREE

    8 ounces (1 cup) ground pork

    4 ounces (½ cup) pork or beef liver

    1 egg, scrambled or soft boiled

    4 ounces (½ cup) steamed or boiled bok choy or Chinese cabbage

    4 ounces (½ cup) cooked zucchini

    4 ounces (½ cup) whole-milk yogurt

Serve meat cooked or raw, combined with the cooked vegetables, eggs, and yogurt. If serving the meat cooked, wait until it has cooled before stirring in the yogurt.

SAMPLE DIET FOUR

    8 ounces (1 cup) canned mackerel or salmon, rinsed and drained

    2 eggs, scrambled or soft boiled

    4 ounces (½ cup) broccoli

    4 ounces (½ cup) kale or other dark leafy green

    4 ounces (½ cup) whole-milk cottage cheese

Cook vegetables and eggs (no need to cook the canned fish, it is already cooked) and mix with the fish. No calcium is needed as mackerel, salmon, and sardines already contain soft, steamed bones, which provide ample calcium.

SUPPLEMENTS

1,400 milligrams calcium, or ¾ teaspoon ground eggshell

1 teaspoon green food, with kelp and spirulina

500 milligrams vitamin C daily per 25 pounds of body weight

100 IU vitamin E daily per 20 pounds of body weight

1,000 milligrams EPA fish or salmon oil daily per ten pounds of
body weight

Chapter Twenty-Five

Diet and Skin Problems

Seeing a dog scratching and itching has become so common that most of us don't even raise an eyebrow. But there are some skin problems that just don't go away by themselves. If an itch persists to the point where you start to notice it really irritating your dog, chances are it needs some attention, whether it's at home or from your vet.

Most dogs will be affected by a skin problem at some time during their lives, be it sudden and temporary, seasonal, or long term, so it's always a good idea to determine the cause so that it can be treated appropriately.

Diagnosis

When it comes to skin problems, diagnosis is often a process of elimination. Often there are numerous causes of itching, redness, and rashes, making an exact diagnosis difficult. If you detect a serious skin problem the first action is to have your veterinarian do a procedure called a skin scraping on the affected areas. A skin scraping can tell you what's present on the skin; most commonly it is yeast, bacteria, or mites. Even if the vet can't pinpoint the original cause, he or she can still tell you what course of action to take. Often the treatment is simple.

If the skin scraping cultures don't show anything, a blood panel and urinalysis can be helpful to see if more serious, underlying health problems are at play.

Causes of Skin Problems

Conditions like hypothyroidism, cushing's disease, and autoimmune disorders can all result in skin problems, so it's important to report any symptoms your dog is showing to your vet. Skin problems can be the result of allergies (both food and environmental), skin parasites (mites and fleas), bacteria, yeast, or a combination of these. Skin issues can be tricky to control, often spreading and causing more problems once the scratching starts. A dog with an allergic reaction, for example, can scratch itself into a yeast problem, sometimes masking the original cause of the itching.

Food and environmental allergies are a likely culprit for your dog's itching and scratching so determining if these are the cause is always a good first step. Environmental and food allergies tend to share symptoms, like face rubbing, ear problems, eye discharge, rashes, redness in the armpit or groin area, and crusty sores.

Treatment

One of the most important things to remember in treating and preventing skin problems is to keep the dog's bedding clean, as well as the yard and flooring in the house. Try to maintain a safe, non-toxic, hygienic environment for your dog. Brushing your dog often helps, too, as does frequent bathing with a non-allergenic shampoo.

To take care of your dog's internal needs, offer a fresh, balanced diet and the right supplements to prevent any internal or digestive problems from showing up on the skin.

If your dog has to take a course of steroids, be on the lookout for yeast symptoms as these drugs can exacerbate yeast problems. If your dog has been prescribed antibiotics, be sure to add probiotics to the diet to keep the good flora and fauna bacteria in the digestive tract, thereby reducing the risk of developing a yeast infection.

Diet

Nutrition plays an important role in preventing and managing skin problems. No matter what the cause of the itching, a balanced, healthy diet can help strengthen your dog's immune system, lessening the chances of skin problems developing.

If you're feeding a commercial diet, always check the label carefully to make sure you're offering good quality animal proteins. Look at the ingredients to avoid cheap fillers, which can cause allergic reactions in some dogs. If you're feeding a homemade diet, try to use foods with only a few ingredients to limit the risk of allergic reactions. Take notice of what your dog may react to, and stick to the foods most suited for your dog. Some food types, like grains, are more likely to cause allergic reactions than others. Sticking to the balanced, varied diets we learned about in "Part II: Feeding Your Dog the Easy Way" will give your dog the best chance of staying strong and healthy. (For more information on offering a balanced, varied diet, see "Part II: Feeding Your Dog the Easy Way." For specific recipes for dogs with yeast and allergy problems, see "Chapter Twenty-Three: Diet and Pancreatitis.")

Supplements

Supplements, in addition to a fresh, balanced diet, are the key to keeping your dog's skin and coat healthy. Regular use of the following supplements can save you a trip to the vet, and save your dog a lot of scratching.

EPA FISH OIL

Fish oil is excellent for the skin and coat, while also boosting the immune system. Offer about one capsule (180 EPA, 120 DHA) daily per ten to twenty pounds of body weight.

PROBIOTIC POWDER

Probiotics are especially helpful for dogs that have been on antibiotics, helping to replace lost digestive flora and fauna. They're also great for fighting yeast infections.

ANTIOXIDANTS

Vitamin C and vitamin E are very important for assisting the immune system. Poor immune function can lead to skin and coat problems.

WITCH HAZEL AND ALOE VERA

Mix a three-to-one solution of witch hazel and aloe vera gel and apply it to the itchy areas as needed. The witch hazel helps temporarily stop the itchiness and kill bacteria, while the aloe vera helps to cool the skin and speed up the healing process.

OATMEAL-BASED SHAMPOO

If your dog is suffering from an environmental allergy it's important to offer regular baths to wash the allergens from the skin. Oatmeal-based shampoos have a drying action to soothe the skin and herbs to help with healing. After bathing, rinse with a solution of half white vinegar and half water to kill the yeast and get rid of any residue. Weekly baths may be necessary until the problem is under control.

Chapter Twenty-Six

Diet and Joint Problems

All of us have seen dogs affected with joint pain and know how difficult it can be for their mobility and comfort. Arthritis and joint pain can be truly debilitating, and many of us think of it as inevitable. But there are some things that can help your dog ease arthritis pain and regain mobility. With the right combination of diet and supplements, there are things that can help ease and reduce the inflammation that causes arthritis pain.

Tommy's Story

A few years ago my Rottweiler, Tommy, began to suffer from elbow and hip dysplasia. His pain caused him to walk with a stilted gait, as if he were an ailing old dog. In a cruel double blow, he was diagnosed with cancer.

Wanting to find him the best treatment, I started to look at how nutrition could affect dogs with cancer. Before coming to live with me Tommy had been raised predominately on dry dog food, with a little fresh food added. When I got him home from the veterinarian visit, I immediately put him on one hundred percent fresh food, cutting the level of carbohydrates he was eating while giving him more animal fat and protein. Within weeks he had improved dramatically, running and playing again with my other dogs.

Though I put him on the diet to help his cancer—and it did, giving him the strength to undergo chemotherapy, which allowed him two years of remission—truly the most remarkable result was the mobility and energy this change in diet gave him.

Treatment

While a number of new prescription drugs on the market offer some relief to dogs suffering from joint problems, many of the drugs also come with unwanted side effects that leave many of us searching for safer alternatives.

There's a lot you can do at home before you have to resort to these medications. In combination with regular veterinarian check-ups, keeping the dog on a regular exercise program is a great way to keep your dog mobile and comfortable. This could include a couple of short walks daily or as much as swimming or chasing a ball. If the dog isn't used to exercise, start with short walks and increase the distance by a small amount each day or as the dog's mobility increases.

Use soft bedding to ease pressure on the joints and make sure your dog has enough shelter and warmth during periods of cold or rough weather.

Diet

After my success with Tommy, I put every dog in my house on a raw diet, taking them off all grains and offering only low-glycemic foods. While a diet low in carbohydrates may not stop joint pain, arthritis, or joint disease from developing, it can greatly improve the quality of dogs' lives by reducing inflammation and allowing them more mobility.

Feeding dogs a diet high in starches and grains can rob them of energy due to longer digestion and lead to further joint pain, so always limit the amount of grains, fruits, and vegetables in the diet. Nightshade vegetables like tomatoes, potatoes, eggplant, and peppers are known to contribute to joint problems, as they cause inflammation, and should be avoided.

Sample Diets for Dogs with Joint Problems

If you've read the diets for dogs with cancer earlier in this section, you'll notice these are pretty similar. Developed from research into cancer-starving nutrition, diets for dogs with joint problems offer the same low-glycemic, high-fat, high-protein foods. They can be served cooked or raw.

For the morning raw meal, feed a variety of high-fat protein sources, alternating between or mixing together any of the foods in the table below. Offer RMBs in the evening.

Figure 26.1. Sample Raw Foods for Dogs with Joint Problems.	
Morning Meal	Evening Meal
Muscle meats like ground beef, lamb, pork, or goat	Chicken necks, wings, backs, and frames
Canned fish like mackerel, salmon, or sardines (packed in water, not oil. Avoid tuna due to the high mercury content.)	Turkey necks
	Beef necks and ribs
Eggs	Pork necks, breast, feet, and tails
Whole-milk yogurt and cottage cheese	Lamb ribs
Organ meats like liver and kidney in small amounts	Rabbit
Heart	
Vegetables, including broccoli, dark leafy greens, cabbage, zucchini, crookneck squash, and bok choy, either cooked or pureed	

Remember, feed these approximate amounts daily:

100-pound dog:	2–3 pounds daily, or two meals of 1–1.5 pounds each
75-pound dog:	1.5–2 pounds daily, or two meals of 12–18 ounces each
50-pound dog:	1–1.5 pounds daily, or two meals of 8–12 ounces each
25-pound dog:	8–12 ounces daily, or two meals of 4–6 ounces each

Sample Daily Cooked Diets for Dogs with Joint Problems

Divide recipes in half for two servings for fifty-pound adult dogs.

SAMPLE DIET ONE

> 8 ounces (1 cup) regular ground beef
>
> 4 ounces (½ cup) beef liver or kidney, cooked with a small amount of butter
>
> 1 egg, raw, scrambled, or soft boiled
>
> 4 ounces (½ cup) steamed or boiled broccoli
>
> 4 ounces (½ cup) cooked yellow crookneck squash
>
> 4 ounces (½ cup) whole-milk yogurt

The meat can be served raw or lightly cooked. Add the fully cooked and mashed vegetables and when cool, add the yogurt.

SAMPLE DIET TWO

> 8 ounces (1 cup) ground chicken
>
> 4 ounces (½ cup) chicken liver, cooked with a small amount of butter
>
> 1 egg, raw, scrambled, or soft boiled
>
> 4 ounces (½ cup) steamed or boiled Spinach
>
> 4 ounces (½ cup) cooked cabbage
>
> 4 ounces (½ cup) cottage cheese

The meat can be served raw or lightly cooked. Add the fully cooked and mashed vegetables and when cool, add the cottage cheese.

SAMPLE DIET THREE

> 8 ounces (1 cup) ground pork
>
> 4 ounces (½ cup) pork or beef liver, cooked with a small amount of butter
>
> 1 egg, raw, scrambled, or soft boiled
>
> 4 ounces (½ cup) steamed or boiled bok choy or Chinese cabbage
>
> 4 ounces (½ cup) zucchini
>
> 4 ounces (½ cup) whole-milk yogurt

The meat can be served raw or lightly cooked. Add the fully cooked and mashed vegetables and when cool, add the yogurt.

SAMPLE DIET FOUR

8 ounces (1 cup) canned mackerel or salmon, rinsed and drained
1 or 2 eggs, raw, scrambled, or soft boiled
4 ounces (½ cup) broccoli
4 ounces (½ cup) kale or other dark leafy green
4 ounces (½ cup) cottage cheese

Combine the fish, fully cooked and mashed vegetables, and cottage cheese. Do not add calcium when serving canned fish, as they include soft, steamed bones, which provide ample calcium.

SUPPLEMENTS

1,400 milligrams calcium or ¾ teaspoon ground eggshell
1 teaspoon green food with kelp, alfalfa, spirulina, and dulce
500 milligrams vitamin C daily per 25 pounds of body weight
100 IU vitamin E daily per 10 pounds of body weight
1,000 milligrams EPA fish or salmon oil daily per ten pounds of
    body weight

Supplements

In addition to a healthy, home prepared diet, using the right supplements can greatly reduce pain and discomfort for a dog with joint problems.

VITAMIN C WITH BIOFLAVONOIDS

In high enough doses vitamin C acts as a pain reliever. Adding bioflavonoids helps with collagen rebuilding and repair. I start at the low end (about 100 milligrams daily per ten pounds of body weight) and slowly increase in weekly intervals. While high doses of vitamin

C with bioflavonoids can help reduce pain, it may cause diarrhea for some. If your dog develops diarrhea, back off to the last lowest dose.

VITAMIN E

Vitamin E works as an antioxidant and in high enough doses (100 IU daily per ten to twenty pounds of body weight) boosts the immune and vascular systems.

EPA FISH OIL

Fish oils are great for reducing inflammation in arthritic dogs.

L-GLUTAMINE

This amino acid helps to slow down muscle atrophy, a common problem with dogs who are too sore to remain active. Give 500 milligrams daily per twenty-five pounds of body weight.

GLUCOSAMINE, CHONDROITIN, AND MANGANESE

Glucosamine eases pain and discomfort, while chondroitin helps rebuild and repair cartilage. Manganese is a mild muscle relaxant that helps get glucosamine and chondroitin to the affected joint areas.

LIQUID YUCCA

Yucca is an effective herbal anti-inflammatory, best administered in its tincture form. Give one drop per ten pounds of body weight, twice daily with meals. Don't give on an empty stomach.

LIQUID WILLOW BARK

Willow bark is the natural form of aspirin. While still a natural product and easier on the stomach than commercially produced aspirin, use only when needed and always give with meals. Do not give willow bark or yucca if your dog is already on non-steroidal anti-inflammatories (NSAIDs). They contain similar properties and cannot be safely given together.

ENZYMES

While some enzymes help with digestion and others help with inflammation, all enzymes are helpful for dogs with joint conditions. Pain and stress often interfere with the absorption of nutrients. Enzymes help the body assimilate nutrients. Helpful enzymes include bromelain and papain.

Chapter Twenty-Seven

Diets for Bladder Health

Diagnosis

Persistent and sometimes difficult to treat, bladder problems can be very painful for your dog. The two main bladder problems, urinary tract infections (UTIs) and urinary tract crystals, tend to share symptoms, which makes diagnosis difficult.

Symptoms

If you notice any of the following symptoms, take your dog to the veterinarian for a complete check-up:

Figure 27.1. Symptoms of Bladder Problems.	
Bladder Problem	Symptoms
Urinary Tract Crystals	Straining to urinate
	Dribbling urine, or urinating only a few drops at a time
	Frequent urination
	Blood in the urine
	Loss of appetite
	Depression
	Occasional vomiting
Urinary Tract Infections	Frequent urination
	Dribbling urine
	Blood in the urine
	Squatting frequently or straining to urinate
	Strong odor to the urine
	Incontinence
	Increased thirst

Getting the right diagnosis is of the utmost importance in these conditions. Your veterinarian can help you determine if these symptoms are a bladder problem or a sign of something more serious, like bladder stones, kidney problems, diabetes, or cushing's disease.

Types of Bladder Problems

In order to know how to treat the different bladder conditions, let's look at each of them in a little more detail.

URINARY TRACT INFECTIONS (UTIS)

While UTIs can occur anywhere within the urinary tract they are most commonly found in the bladder. More common among female dogs, they can be hard to detect, sometimes producing few obvious symptoms.

If your dog is diagnosed with a UTI, the veterinarian will usually perform a standard blood panel and a urinalysis. The urinalysis indicates how well the dog is concentrating the urine and if there is blood, protein, or bacteria present in the urine. Be sure to ask for a Sterile Urine Culture, in which urine is taken in a sterile manner and sent to a laboratory to culture. This will indicate the exact bacteria present, and the correct antibiotic to use to get rid of the infection. Be sure to let these antibiotics run their entire course. Repeat the sterile urine culture once the dog has been off antibiotics for ten days as UTIs can be difficult to clear up.

URINARY TRACT CRYSTALS

Mineral and stone deposits that accumulate in the urinary tract can form crystals. These can come in many shapes and sizes. A recent study found that almost half the normal, healthy dogs tested had a few crystals present in their tracts, so chances are that your dog will experience them at some time during his or her life. Many dogs have crystals present in their urine and remain healthy and symptom-free. Always have a veterinarian do a complete examination of your dog if you suspect crystals or stones—left unchecked, they can cause a potentially life-threatening blockage in the urinary tract. In severe cases crystals grow to the point where they fill the bladder, requiring surgery. In many cases they can be treated with antibiotics after your vet performs a urinalysis.

The two most common types of crystals are struvites and oxalate crystals. Each of these crystals causes the pH balance in the body to change, so checking the pH value of the urine is a good way to determine which type of crystals are present and what treatment is appropriate. You can get pH testing kits from any good health store or pharmacy.

Two less common types of crystals and stones are called purine and cystine.

STRUVITE CRYSTALS

Struvite crystals often form in dogs with UTIs, and like UTIs, these crystals are more common in females. Struvites are almost always accompanied by bacteria that create a high alkaline pH. To get rid of struvite crystals, the first thing you need to do is to get your vet to diagnose and treat the infection. It is important when struvites are found in the urine, to have a sterile urine culture and sensitivity test done to determine what bacteria are present since different types of bacteria respond only to specific antibiotics.

CALCIUM OXALATE CRYSTALS

Calcium Oxalate crystals, the second most common type, tend to affect more males than females and often are caused by a genetic predisposition in some breeds to form stones if left untreated. Like struvites, these crystals can also be found in healthy dogs with no other symptoms and these will often show acidic (low) pH levels. While surgery may be necessary to remove the stones caused by crystal accumulation, a combination of supplements and alkalizing foods in the diet can help.

PURINE CRYSTALS AND STONES

This is another inherited condition, most commonly seen in Dalmatians and Bulldogs. Dogs with this condition are unable to process foods high in purines. Unfortunately, the foods highest in purines are red meat, organ meats, and certain types of fish. The animal-based foods with the lowest purine content are eggs and dairy. Always consult with your veterinarian if you suspect your dog may have this problem, as medical diagnosis and guidance is necessary. Diets need to be low in purine while still containing enough animal protein for good health. The Dalmatian Club of America has good information on purines and offers a wealth of information on their website (www.thedca.org/purines.html).

CYSTINE CRYSTALS AND STONES

Called cystinuria, this is an inherited condition caused by a defect in the kidneys. When stones occur, medical attention is of the utmost importance because the stones can cause blockage of the urinary tract and need to be surgically removed. Acidic urine is a sign of this condition and treatment options and diets are still being researched. For more information, refer to Christie Keith's wonderful website and email list (www.caninecystinuria.com/Treatment.html).

INCONTINENCE

Incontinence is another problem associated with bladder conditions. If you notice signs of incontinence, always get a urine culture and sensitivity test done. If the tests come up clear, your dog probably has a true incontinence issue, a problem common to senior dogs and spayed females. Diet changes that may improve bladder control include removing grains and starches such as potatoes, sweet potatoes, winter squash, rice, oats, corn, and all types of grain. An herb called corn-silk, which can often be found in a liquid tincture, may also improve urinary tract tone.

Treatment

Most of the treatments for bladder problems will come from your vet, but that's not to say you can't take responsibility for keeping your dog's bladder in excellent shape. Whether your dog is recovering from a bladder problem or you just want to make sure he or she doesn't get one, try to remember the following tips:

- Water consumption is the single most important factor in preventing bladder problems, so make sure your dog always has access to fresh water.
- Encourage your dog to drink. Keeping the kidneys and bladders flushed is the easiest way to keep crystals and stones from forming.
- Feed moist fresh-food diets, either raw or cooked.
- Don't keep your dog confined if you can help it, and make sure he or she is always able to urinate when the need arises. Frequent urination (once every four hours or so) lets the dog flush out any built-up crystals and also prevents crystals from forming.
- Check the minerals in your water supply, especially if you have hard water in your area.
- Distilled water is a good choice if you suspect your own water supply isn't suitable, as it can help prevent some cases of stone and crystal formation.
- If your dog has been treated for a bladder problem, continue follow-ups with your vet.
- Try to have your dog retested with a sterile urine culture a week or so after finishing treatment to make sure the infection is gone.
- Always keep an eye out for any symptoms of bladder conditions. The sooner these are managed, the less chance there is of complications arising.

Diet

Despite the claims of the prescription diets on the market, they won't cure a UTI or struvite crystals, nor will a change in kibble. Treatment with the proper antibiotic will help clear up struvite crystals by getting rid of the bacteria that causes the high pH level. To give your dog the best chance of a full recovery, and keep the problem from reoccurring, keep up with the fresh-food diets we learned about in "Part II: Feeding Your Dog the Easy Way," with a particular focus on high-moisture foods like chicken broth, yogurt, soup, and cottage cheese.

Acid and Alkaline in the Diet

STRUVITES

If your dog has struvite bladder stones, then acidifying the diet, along with treating the infection can help dissolve the stones. Try offering ascorbic acid (a form of vitamin C) and distilled water. Both can help prevent the formation of stones. This treatment has not, however, been found to be effective for cystinuria.

The easiest way to keep the urine pH balance acidic is to feed more acidic foods (meats, dairy, and most grains) than alkaline foods (most fruits and vegetables). Any fresh raw diet is naturally high in acidic foods.

Too Alkaline?

Remember, the most accurate way to determine pH in the urine is by testing the first catch of the day since pH levels vary a great deal within a twenty-four-hour period.

Figure 27.2. Acidic Foods.		
Acidic foods		
Chicken	Fish	Rice (brown and white)
Beef	Pork	Beans
Eggs	Cottage cheese	Nuts
Yogurt	All seafood	

Keep in mind that alkaline pH and struvite crystals are usually caused by infections and not an alkaline diet. Trying to make the urine more acidic, while it may prevent more crystals from forming, will not get rid of the infection. Always seek treatment from your vet when treating an infection.

Calcium Oxalate

Unlike struvites, diet changes can be helpful for dogs prone to oxalates. The primary foods that contain oxalates are grains and vegetables. Since the primary ingredients of commercial dog foods are grains, the best way to achieve a good diet is to offer a home-prepared diet. This way, you can monitor the ingredients of the food your dog is eating.

Foods to avoid include barley, corn, brown rice, what, soy, most beans, potatoes, sweet potatoes, spinach, and nuts.

Foods that can be fed include all meat, dairy (no flavoring or sweeteners and not soy-based), eggs, Brussels sprouts, cauliflower, white rice, canned pumpkin, and meat and fish broths. Sources vary on assessing the oxalate content in food and many charts are available on the Internet comparing these amounts.

A good proportion to feed would be approximately sixty-five to seventy-five percent animal protein and twenty-five to thirty-five percent carbohydrate (from the vegetables listed above or white rice).

Approximate feeding amounts are two to three percent of the dog's body weight daily. On average, a 100-pound dog would get two to three pounds of food daily (approximately four to six cups), a fifty-pound dog would get one to one and a half pounds daily (two to three cups), a twenty-five pound dog would get eight to twelve ounces (one to one and a half cups), and a twelve-pound dog would get six to eight ounces (three quarters to one cup) per day. Calcium should be added at a rate of about 900 milligrams per pound of food served.

Calcium can be another issue for calcium oxalate formers. While it is uncertain whether or not calcium will create problems, it is known that calcium excretion in the urine can form crystals and stones, so it is a good idea to avoid high-calcium foods. Additionally, medications such as steroids and furosemid (lasix), can cause calcium excretion in the urine and may need to be avoided. You may add some yogurt or cottage cheese to the diet, but only in small amounts. You will need to supplement calcium (calcium citrate is preferred for oxalate formers), but use a supplement without vitamin D as vitamin D increases the absorption of calcium.

Meat suggestions include ground beef, ground chicken, ground turkey, ground pork, baked white fish, beef, chicken, pork or turkey heart, and lamb.

Carbohydrates to use include white rice, Brussels sprouts, canned pumpkin, green peas, white cabbage, zucchini, acorn squash, bok choy, melon, and egg noodles. Be sure to boil all vegetables and rice before serving. Cooking is thought to reduce some of the oxalate content, and raw vegetables contain a higher oxalate value on most oxalate food level charts.

You may vary the meat choices in these recipes for variety. The same would apply for the smaller ratio of carbohydrate choices. Use at least three different primary protein sources for a week's worth of meals.

Remember, feed these approximate amounts daily:

100-pound dog:	2–3 pounds daily, or two meals of 1–1.5 pounds each
75-pound dog:	1.5–2 pounds daily, or two meals of 12–18 ounces each
50-pound dog:	1–1.5 pounds daily, or two meals of 8–12 ounces each
25-pound dog:	8–12 ounces daily, or two meals of 4–6 ounces each

Sample Diets for Dogs with Calcium Oxalate Crystals and Stones

Below are sample daily cooked diets for fifty-pound adult dogs. Divide recipes in half for two servings.

SAMPLE DIET ONE

12 ounces (1½ cups) cooked ground beef

2 eggs, lightly scrambled or hard boiled

8 ounces (1 cup) steamed and mashed cauliflower

2 tablespoons whole-milk yogurt

Combine the meat, egg, and cauliflower. When cool, add the yogurt.

SAMPLE DIET TWO

12 ounces (1½ cups) cooked chicken breast

4 ounces (½ cup) chicken heart

4 ounces (½ cup) white rice

2 tablespoons cottage cheese

Combine the chicken, chicken heart, and rice. When cool, add the cottage cheese.

Supplements

There are a great range of supplements available these days to help support your dog's bladder and urinary tract.

VITAMIN B COMPLEX

Giving your dog a vitamin B complex helps fight urinary infection and maintain kidney health. Give a full dose for large dogs, half dose for medium-sized dogs and a quarter of a dose for small dogs.

ASCORBIC ACID/VITAMIN C

Given in high enough quantities, ascorbic acid, a type of vitamin C, can help dissolve stones.

CRANBERRY JUICE CAPSULES

If your vet confirms that the infection is gone, give your dog a daily dose of cranberry juice capsules. These are great for preventing new bacteria from adhering to the bladder wall. Always wait until you have the vet's all clear, as these capsules won't help if bacteria are already present.

ANTIOXIDANTS

Antioxidants such as vitamin C and vitamin E are great for boosting your dog's immune system.

EPA FISH OIL

EPA fish oil is another great helper as it keeps the immune system strong and helps prevent inflammation. Give 1,000 milligrams daily per ten to twenty pounds of the dog's body weight.

COQ10

COQ10 is another great supplement, particularly useful with kidney stones.

CORNSILK

Cornsilk, available as an herbal tincture, can be helpful in some cases of incontinence. It can be given daily as needed.

PROBIOTIC POWDER

Probiotics help replace some of the beneficial bacteria that antibiotics destroy. Use probiotics in between doses of antibiotics, not at the same time as antibiotics are being given. Continue the use of the probiotics for several weeks or months after a course of antibiotics.

Chapter Twenty-Eight

Diet and Gastric Problems

Most dogs have experienced diarrhea or vomiting at one time or another. These are usually short-term events, but if these symptoms linger always seek the advice of a veterinarian. Persistent vomiting or diarrhea can cause dehydration and even malnutrition. Feeding the right diet, with some helpful supplements, can help alleviate these symptoms and get your dog back on track.

Symptoms

The symptoms of gastric problems are usually fairly easy to spot. A dog suffering a gastric problem will usually show signs of:

- Vomiting
- Diarrhea
- Poor appetite
- Insatiable hunger
- Weight loss
- Coat and skin problems

Some symptoms, like diarrhea and vomiting, tend to show up soon after the gastric problem appears. Others, like skin and coat problems, happen further down the line, usually when problems in the digestive tract have hampered the dog's ability to assimilate the nutrients in their food properly. So what's causing these problems?

Causes of Gastric Problems

Inflammation of the intestines is the most common cause of gastric distress. You can usually tell which intestine is affected by the symptoms—irritation and inflammation in the small intestine tend to cause vomiting, whereas large intestine issues usually result in loose stools and diarrhea. Sometimes a dog will exhibit both of these symptoms, indicating that both areas are affected.

Spasms in the digestive tract are another common cause of gastric complaints. Often resulting in pain and loose stools, spasms can increase inflammation in the digestive tract and interfere with a dog's ability to absorb nutrients from food. Left untreated this can lead to a whole range of problems.

Why do gastric disorders affect some dogs and not others? Good question. There's no one answer everyone agrees on. Some researchers think a poor immune system is the culprit, while others blame autoimmune disorders, food allergies, or even hyperactivity and anxiety. If you notice any of these symptoms, it's important to take your dog to the veterinarian immediately for a proper diagnosis.

Diagnosis

Blood work and physical examinations, which are the two most common tests vets use to diagnose canine health problems, don't always pick up gastric disorders. Fecal tests are important to check for parasites. Blood work can reveal evidence of certain problems such as SIBO (small intestinal overgrowth), EPI (exocrine pancreatic insufficiency), or HGE (hemorrhagic gastroenteritis). Occasionally an endoscopy, which takes a sample from the small intestine, will be needed.

If the sample shows inflammation it can often mean inflammatory bowel disease (IBD). However, there are a number of other problems whose symptoms mimic those of IBD, like parasites, hyperthyroidism, bacterial infections, and liver disease, so it's important to rule these out first in order to be sure that you're dealing with IBD.

Some other gastric diagnoses include:

SMALL INTESTINAL BACTERIA OVERGROWTH (SIBO)

This is a bacterial overgrowth that is becoming more common in dogs. This problem creates large, gassy stools with weight loss and often appetite loss. This is diagnosed by measuring the bacteria count in the duodenal fluid by endoscope and finding an elevation of serum folate and a low level of serum cobalamin. This disorder is treated with antibiotics and reduced-fat diets.

EXOCRINE PANCREATIC INSUFFICIENCY (EPI)

This is a condition in which the pancreas does not secrete the proper enzymes to digest foods. This is found commonly in German Shepherds, although it is seen in other breeds as well. Testing is needed to diagnose this disorder, and prescription enzyme medications are needed for treatment. Like SIBO, EPI results in large, smelly stools. These are grey in color, often with a greasy texture.

Symptoms of EPI include increased appetite and fluffy, huge, smelly, greasy, gray-colored stools, loss of weight, gas, loud stomach noises, etc. The dog's pancreas doesn't produce enough digestive enzymes to break the food down and therefore, no matter how much they eat, they can't digest their food and they start to starve to death. Loss of weight is fast. Like SIBO, dogs with EPI will also have increased serum folate and decreased serum cobalamin, but a test called TLI (trypsin like immunoreactivity) will determine if it is EPI. These dogs often need pancreatic enzymes, along with low-fiber, easily digested fats.

HEMORRHAGIC GASTROENTERITIS (HGE)

With hemorrhagic gastroenteritis, there is bloody diarrhea which is often red and clotted in appearance. Vomiting and lethargy can develop later. A high-packed cell volume (PCV) in a blood panel will confirm the diagnosis. Toy breeds are more at risk, but HGE has good recovery outcomes. Treatment often includes antibiotics and trying new protein sources, as there is some belief it may be caused by food allergies.

In most cases the diagnosis won't be that serious, and can be as simple as a reaction to eating too much food or to a certain food.

Treatment

While many gastric complaints can be easily fixed through the right combination of diet and supplements, some do require veterinarian care and medications. Once the symptoms have been treated, it is time to look at the diet and possible supplements to help maintain good digestion.

There are also a lot of safe, effective products on the market these days, with few side effects. Originally developed for human patients, these products are designed to help with digestion and assimilation, while soothing irritation and bringing down inflammation. They are equally suitable for short- and long-term treatment.

Digestive Enzymes

Dogs with irritated or inflamed digestive tracts have difficulty breaking down food and absorbing the nutrients, which makes digestive enzymes particularly useful. Digestive enzymes are also helpful for healing the digestive tract and preventing gas.

There are several types of digestive enzymes, each designed to help break down certain types of food. Bromelain, which is derived from pineapple, is perhaps the most effective enzyme for canines. It is one of a number of plant enzymes that help fight inflammation and reduce swelling. However, the most important digestive enzymes for food digestion problems in dogs are animal-based enzymes, specifically pancreatin and pancrealipase. These help predigest fat and proteins in the stomach, easing digestion in the small intestine. The best way to offer these is in a blend like Berte's Zymes. For more information, see the "Supplements" section at the end of this chapter.

Friendly Bacteria

Antibiotics tend to destroy the good bacteria along with the bad, so it's always a good idea to help your dog replace some of those good bacteria after treatment. Replacing important flora and fauna like aci-dophilus, streptococcus, and enterococcus helps strengthen digestion and boost the immune system, while preventing gas, spasms, and dis-comfort. Friendly bacteria also help to fight yeast overgrowth and maintain a balance in the digestive tract.

L-Glutamine

L-glutamine is an amino acid that can help speed up healing in the digestive system while repairing muscles and intestinal tissue. It also induces the large intestine to remove excess water, which is helpful for dogs prone to diarrhea.

N-Acetyl Glucosamine (NAG)

Dogs, like humans, need NAG to help line their digestive tract. Dogs with gastric complaints often can't produce enough NAG, which slows their digestion and healing. Studies have shown that patients given NAG were able to turn the problem around, replacing the digestive lining while repairing damaged tissue.[13]

Fish and Marine Oils

One of nature's best anti-inflammatories, fish oil is great for patients with digestive disorders.[14] Fish oil also helps regulate the immune system, which can help with IBD and other gastric upsets.

Diet

For many years the common wisdom for dogs with gastric disorders has been to offer high-fiber or hypoallergenic diets. While some of these high-fiber treatments can help improve stool production and reduce vomiting, they lack the nutrition your dog really needs to heal and are, at best, a temporary solution. High-fiber foods help remove excess moisture in the large intestine, which makes for more normal looking stool. It is what you don't see, however, that is more important than what you do—such diets continue to irritate the intestinal tract, hampering the immune system and causing further problems down the line. Far from a long-term solution, most dogs tend to relapse once these treatments are stopped.

Almost all commercial dog foods, whether premium, hypoallergenic or prescription brand, are high in fiber and grains, and tend to burden the dog's digestion leading to gassiness, spasms, and discomfort in the intestinal tract.

Home-cooked and raw fresh-food diets are the best option for dogs with gastric problems as they are easier to digest and absorb. Feeding your dog at home allows you to reduce the fiber content in the meals to amounts your dog can tolerate while removing any foods that your dog may have difficulty digesting.

The best raw diets for dogs with gastric problems are those that contain RMBs, which help keep the stools firm. If you're feeding a cooked diet, offer your dog easily digested fiber sources like pulped or pureed vegetables. Vegetables from the cruciferous family like cabbage and broccoli are great for healing the digestive tract, and are safe to offer every day.

Dogs with gastric problems still need fat in their diets, but to make sure they are digested well offer fresh fats that are either raw or lightly cooked.

Remember, feed these approximate amounts daily:

100-pound dog:	2–3 pounds daily, or two meals of 1–1.5 pounds each
75-pound dog:	1.5–2 pounds daily, or two meals of 12–18 ounces each
50-pound dog:	1–1.5 pounds daily, or two meals of 8–12 ounces each
25-pound dog:	8–12 ounces daily, or two meals of 4–6 ounces each

Sample Diets for Dogs with Gastric Problems

The best overall diet for dogs with gastric upsets should be high-protein, medium-fat with limited carbohydrates and fiber. You may want to start with four small meals per day (break each meal in half) and slowly move to two meals a day over the course of a few weeks.

Here are sample diets for fifty-pound adult dogs with gastric problems. Each recipe is for one day; divide into two (or four) portions as desired.

SAMPLE DIET ONE (COOKED)

> 16 ounces (2 cups) meat, either raw or lightly cooked lean ground beef, beef heart, baked white fish, or canned mackerel or salmon that has been drained and rinsed
>
> 8 ounces (1 cup) pulped vegetables, preferably cabbage, broccoli, celery, dark leafy greens, mustard, turnip greens, or spinach, thoroughly cooked and mashed
>
> 1 egg, soft boiled or scrambled
>
> 2 tablespoons plain yogurt

SAMPLE DIET TWO (RAW)

Morning meal

> 4 or 5 chicken necks (raw, with the skin removed) or two chicken backs (skin removed) or four chicken wings (skin removed)

Evening meal

> 12 ounces (1½ cups) lean meat, such as cut up beef heart, skinless turkey breast, skinless white meat chicken, canned salmon or mackerel that has been rinsed and drained.

If you're feeding a cooked diet, offer variations of the first meal and add calcium at 900 milligrams per pound of food served. The vegetables are added for fiber, which helps firm the stool. The raw diet gets calcium from the bone and the bone, which also offers fiber for keeping the stool firm. Remember to add l-glutamine at 500 milligrams daily per 20 pounds of body weight, digestive enzymes with pancreatin and pancrealipase, and probiotics to help heal the digestive tract and reduce inflammation.

Gastric Remedies

In addition to these diets, here are a couple of great remedies for diarrhea and vomiting, two of the most common symptoms of digestive complaints:

DIARRHEA REMEDY

If your dog is suffering from diarrhea, try giving some plain canned pumpkin to help your dog form firm stools. Dogs weighing up to thirty pounds will need half a teaspoon, thirty- to sixty-pound dogs need one teaspoon, and bigger dogs should get between two teaspoons and one tablespoon.

VOMITING REMEDY

Cabbage is great for settling a troubled stomach. Boil some cabbage for about fifteen to twenty minutes and let it cool. Give two milliliters of the liquid (one teaspoon is equal to five milliliters) per ten pounds of body weight as needed.

Supplements

Now let's take a look at how to offer your dog some of the natural treatments mentioned earlier in this chapter.

BERTE'S ZYME

A great help for digestion and relief of inflammation, Berte's Zyme also helps your dog regain weight after periods of illness. Give small dogs half a tablet with each meal, medium dogs one tablet, and large dogs two tablets.

BERTE'S DIGESTION BLEND

This blend is excellent for all types of gastric and stomach disorders, helping get your dog's digestion and assimilation of nutrients back on track. Give half a teaspoon per meal for small dogs, one teaspoon for medium dogs, and two teaspoons for large dogs.

BERTE'S GREEN BLEND

Berte's Green Blend, high in vitamin B and minerals, is easy to absorb and a great immune booster.

ANTIOXIDANTS

Dogs with IBD often have difficulty absorbing antioxidants, making regular supplementation important. Supplement your dog's diet regularly with vitamin C, bioflavonoids, vitamin E, and zinc.

Bud's Story

One of my Rottweilers, Bud, was diagnosed with IBD when he was three years old. Not wanting to play ping-pong with pharmaceuticals, I put him on a low-fiber raw diet similar to the sample diet above, adding a number of enzymes and other digestive supplements, for one year. It worked. In the second year, as his condition improved, we were able to greatly reduce the supplement doses.

Bud did not have a relapse for eight years after his change in diet. To boost his immune system, I gave him the Berte's Immune Blend for the antioxidants, digestive enzymes, l-glutamine, and probiotics, and fish oil capsules to help with inflammation and to strengthen his immune system. And it wasn't only Bud who did well on this diet; I've had great success supplementing and feeding other dogs this way. More recently, I have developed the Berte's Digestion Blend, which contains l-glutamine, probiotics, digestive enzymes, N-acetyl glucosamine (NAG), and ginger (to help control nausea).

Chapter Twenty-Nine

Diet and the Immune System

The dog's immune system works hard, constantly fighting the insults of daily life from pollutants to viruses and bacteria. It makes sense, then, that when such an important system starts to malfunction a lot can go wrong, making immune supportive nutrition critical to your dog's health.

Symptoms

When a dog's immune system breaks down, it leaves the dog's body defenseless, open to everything from colds to cancer. The first signs, though, are usually not that serious. They include:

- Dry flaking skin
- Thinning coat
- Running teary eyes
- Excessive foot licking
- Hot spots
- Chronic diarrhea
- Hyperactivity
- Inability to gain weight
- Mood swings

Diagnosis

If you see any of the above symptoms, be sure to head to your vet. Though these symptoms can be signs of different problems, like fleas, dermatitis, or allergies, they often point to disorders of the immune system, which can become quite serious if not treated properly.

Types and Causes of Immune Problems

There are two main types of immune system disorders, each of them corresponding to different levels of function in the system.

An underactive immune system occurs when the immune system is suppressed. An overactive immune system, on the other hand, is one that has become confused and starts to attack the body.

It can often be difficult to determine which cause is at play, so be sure to seek out an exact diagnosis from your vet. If your vet suspects an immune disorder he will most likely conduct a urinalysis and a blood panel to see which type your dog has and how far along it is.

Underactive Immune System

Often when a dog's immune system is suppressed it starts to under-perform, making it difficult for the dog to fight off bacteria and viruses. A number of things can compromise your dog's immune system, such as:

- Vaccinations (especially during a bitch's heat cycle or during pregnancy)
- Antibiotics
- Steroids or other immune-suppressing drugs
- Protein malnutrition
- Insufficient calories
- Vitamin or mineral deficiencies
- Hormonal fluctuations
- Virus
- Disease
- Illnesses and systemic diseases like diabetes, renal failure, systemic lupus erthematosus, and neoplasia
- Hypothyroidism

More prone to infections and ill health, dogs with underactive immune systems are often unable to protect themselves against the effects of common environmental pollutants like pesticides and herbicides, leading to further problems. Left untreated, an underactive immune system can leave a dog susceptible to more serious ailments like cancer, contagious disorders like leptospirosis and tick borne diseases, and urinary tract infections.

Overactive Immune System

Otherwise known as autoimmune disease, an overactive immune system is when the body overreacts to normal agents found in the body and creates antigens to destroy them. With the immune system in "overdrive," the body begins to destroy the good with bad, in some cases killing normal red blood cells.

In the short term an overactive immune system can lead to symptoms of allergic response like hot spots, skin problems, and teary eyes. Left untreated, serious conditions like arthritis, inflammatory bowel disease, and reproductive problems can develop.

One of the main dangers of an overactive immune system is that it can lead to the development of other autoimmune disorders, further compromising your pet's health.

Autoimmune Disorders

Autoimmune disorders come in two types—congenital (inherited) and acquired (developed during the dog's life). Stress, drug reactions, poor nutrition, and exposure to chemicals can all lead to acquired autoimmune disorders.

Treatment

Many of the traditional treatments for immune problems work by suppressing the immune system. While these treatments offer temporary relief, they can cause more problems later on. Often when the treatments are finished the symptoms return, and in many cases are

Figure 29.1. Common Autoimmune Disorders in Dogs.	
Thyroiditis	Rheumatoid Arthritis
Vitiligo	Diabetes Mellitus
Addison's Disease	Seizures
Cushing's Syndrome	Myasthenia Gravis
Hemolytic Anemia	Hypogonadism
Systemic Lupus Erythematosus (SLE)	Connective Tissue Disease
Chronic Active Hepatitis	Glomerulonephritis
Uveitis	Alopecia
Intestinal Lymphagiectasia	Graves' Disease
Thrombocytopenic Purpura	Buck

> If for some reason it's absolutely necessary to give your dog immune suppressive treatment, be sure to offer a nutritious immune-supportive diet to counteract any possible side effects.

worse than before. Antibiotics, for example, indiscriminately kill all bacteria including the essential friendly kinds in the digestive system, further compromising the immune system.

Other conventional treatments for immune system problems tend to treat the symptoms rather than the cause. Dry dog foods, special shampoos, and cortisone and other steroids, all administered in an attempt to get the dog's immune system back on track, are often offer only temporary improvement. So what can you do?

- Limit your dog's exposure to common chemicals like pesticides, herbicides, and household cleaners. Dogs are lower to the ground, which means they're in closer contact with the many potentially dangerous chemicals used in the home and the yard.

- Always offer the freshest, most balanced diets you can, along with immune-supportive supplements.
- If you do need to treat a diagnosed immune system problem, take a look at the "Supplements" section later in this chapter for information on how to boost your dog's immune function naturally.
- Only vaccinate if and when your dog is in perfect health—over-vaccination can lead to immune complications.
- Always make sure to give your dog plenty of physical exercise.
- Use common sense to limit the stress in your dog's daily life. If your dog is a working or show dog, this means balancing performance and training with time to relax at home. Keeping your dog happy will go a long way to preventing immune problems in the first place.

Diet

A fresh-food diet, whether raw or cooked, is the dog's best defense against any immune problem. Fresh foods, as we know, offer the dog more readily available nutrients. These nutrients help to create and maintain a strong immune system and free up energy to fight invading bacteria and viruses. Dry dog foods, on the other hand, are harder to digest and can cause the immune system to develop antigens in response to the processed ingredients.

The best cure is always prevention, so offer a varied and balanced diet, rich in proteins, fats, and nutrients. In combination with immune supportive supplements, you'll be giving your dog the best chance of a healthy, full life.

Supplements

The last thing a dog with a compromised immune system needs is harsh medicines. Try offering a combination of these natural immune-enhancing supplements to get your dog's defenses back to full strength.

ANTIOXIDANTS

Vitamins A, C, and E, along with the minerals selenium and beta-carotene, are powerful antioxidants, great for destroying the free radicals that can attack your dog when his or her immune system is down. Linoleic acid and bioflavonoids with quercitin can be great for boosting underactive immune systems, too. If your dog is having immune troubles offer these daily.

ZINC

Dogs with underactive immune systems are often zinc-deficient. In consultation with your vet, offer your dog a regular zinc supplement.

B VITAMINS

B complex vitamins promote good nerve and brain function and can ease stress. B6 is particularly helpful for dogs with underactive immune systems.

PROBIOTICS AND DIGESTIVE ENZYMES

Often dogs with compromised immune function also have problems with digestion and utilization of the food they eat. These supplements help to predigest fats and proteins in the stomach, enhancing the absorption of nutrients.

FISH OILS

Fish body oils are great for bringing down any inflammation while regulating and promoting immune function.

IMMUNE-BOOSTING HERBS

If you're looking for a natural alternative to synthesized drugs, there are a number of great immune-supporting herbal blends on the market. Some of the best include echinacea, goldenseal, red clover, dandelion, burdock, cats claw, essiac tea, suma, and astralagus. Administer these in a glycerine-based tincture whenever possible.

Notes

Part I: Nutrition Basics

[1] Brady, D. and Palmeri, C. August 6, 2007. "The Pet Economy," *Business Week* www.businessweek.com/magazine/content/07_32/b4045001.htm.

[2] American Pet Products Manufacturers Association. 2007. "Industry Statistics & Trendswww.appma.org/press_industrytrends.asp.

[3] The Kennel Club. 2006. "The History of Crufts," www.thekennelclub.org.uk/item/256.

[4] Thurston, Mary Elizabeth. 1996. *The Lost History of the Canine Race: Our 15,000-Year Love Affair with the Dog.* Kansas City, MO: Andrews and McMeel Publishing. 4.

[5] Ibid. 11.

[6] Ibid. 5–6.

[7] Ibid. 7–8.

[8] Sugimura, T. 2000. "Nutrition and dietary carcinogens," *Carcinogenesis,* 21.3: 387–95.

[9] Pavia, Audrey. July 1996. "History of Premium Dry Dog Food," PetProduct News, 50.7: 1–3.

[10] Kronfeld, D.S., PhD, DSc, MVSc. 1972. *Canine Nutrition.* Philadelphia, PA: University of Pennsylvania, School of Veterinary Medicine. Preface.

[11] Ibid.

[12] Op. Cit. Thurston. 12–14.

[13] National Academy of Sciences, Subcommittee on Dog Nutrition, Committee on Animal Nutrition. 1974 "Nutrient Requirement of Dogs." Washington DC.

[14] Sheffy, B.E. 1989. "The 1985 Revision of the National Research Council Nutrient Requirements of Dogs and Its Impact on the Pet Food Industry," *Nutrition of the Dog and Cat.* Cambridge, MA: Cambridge University Press. 18–19.

[15] Ibid. 19.

[16] Ibid. 25.

[17] Canadian Veterinarian Medical Association, "A Common Sense Guide to Feeding Your Dog or Cat," www.cvma-acmv.org/petfood/feed12.htm.

[18] Pet Food Institute, "A Well Nourished Pet is a Happy Companion," www.pfionline.org/nutrition.htm.

[19] *Nexus Magazine*. October/November 2007. "Junk Pet Food and the Damage Done," 14.6.

[20] Brown, Steve and Taylor, Beth. 2005. *See Spot Live Longer*. Creekobear Press.

[21] Kronfeld, D.S., PhD, DSc, MVSc. July/August 1982. "Protein Quality and Amino Acid Profiles of Commercial Dog Foods," *Journal of the American Hospital Association,* 18: 682–83.

[22] Kronfeld, D.S., PhD, DSc, MVSc. June 1978. "Home Cooking for Dogs, Food Energy-Carbohydrates, Fats and Proteins," *American Kennel Club Gazette.* 64.

[23] Finco, D.R., Brown, S.A., Crowell, W.A., Brown, C.A., Barsanti, J.A., Carey, D.P., and Hirakawa, D.A. September 1994. "Effects of aging and dietary protein intake on uninephrectomized geriatric dogs," *Am J Vet Res.* 1282–90. www.ncbi.nlm.nih.gov/entrez/query.fcgi?cmd=Retrieve&db=PubMed&list _uids=7802397&dopt=Abstract.

[24] Laflamme, Dottie, DVM, Ph.D. "Nutritional Needs Of Older Dogs," http://pets.yahoo.com/pets/dogs/hn/nutritional_needs_of_older_dogs.

[25] Purina. "Demystifying Myths About Protein," http://164.109.18.227/dogs/puppies.asp?article=471.

[26] Kronfeld, DS, PhD, DSc, MVSc. 1972. "Some Nutritional Problems in Dogs," *Canine Nutrition*. Philadelphia, PA: University of Pennsylvania, School of Veterinary Medicine. 32–33.

[27] Case, Linda P., MS, Carey, Daniel P.D., DVM, and Hirakawa, Diane A., PhD, 1995. *Canine and Feline Nutrition*. Mosby Press. 17–18.

[28] Kronfeld, DS., PhD, DSC, MVSC. July 1978. "Home Cooking for Dogs, The Staples, Meat, Meat By-Products and Cereal," *American Kennel Club Gazette,* 55.

[29] Op. Cit. Case, Carey, Hirakawa. 17–18.

[30] Op. Cit Kronfeld. "Home Cooking for Dogs, Food Energy-Carbohydrates, Fats and Proteins." 62.

[31] Op. Cit Kronfeld. "Home Cooking for Dogs, The Staples, Meat, Meat by-Products and Cereal." 55.

[32] Op. Cit. Kronfeld. "Home Cooking for Dogs, Food Energy-Carbohydrates, Fats and Proteins." 62.

[33] Armand, W.B., VMD. 1972. "Diet and Gastrointestinal Problems," *Canine Nutrition*. Philadelphia, PA: University of Pennsylvania, School of Veterinary Medicine. 49.

[34] Op. Cit Kronfeld. "Home Cooking for Dogs, The Staples, Meat, Meat by-Products and Cereal." 55.

[35] Op. Cit. Case, Carey, Hirakawa. 17–18.

[36] Op. Cit Kronfeld. "Home Cooking for Dogs, The Staples, Meat, Meat by-Products and Cereal." 55.

[37] Kienzle, E., and Meyer, H. 1989. "The Effects of Carbohydrate-Free Diets Containing Different Levels of Protein on Reproduction in the Bitch," *Nutrition of the Dog and Cat*. Cambridge, MA: Cambridge University Press. 254–25.

[38] Kendall, Robert V., PhD. 1997. "Therapeutic Nutrition for the Cat, Dog and Horse," *Complementary and Alternative Veterinary Medicine*. Mosby Press. 62.

[39] Bauer, John E. DVM, PhD, DACVn. Essential fatty acid metabolism in dogs and cats, College of Veterinary Medicine, Texas A&M University, College Station, TX 77843-4474 USA.

[40] "Simpson, JW SDA BVM Mphil MRCVS, Anderson, RS BVMS PhD MRCVS and Markwell, PJ Bsc, BvetMed MRCVS. 1993. *Clinical Nutrition of the Dog and Cat*. Blackwell Scientific Publications. 66–70.

[41] Op. Cit. Kronfeld, D.S., PhD, DSc, MVSc. "Home Cooking for the Dog." 60–61.

[42] **Supplement table references**

Balch, James F., and Balch, Phyllis A. 1990. *Prescription for Nutritional Healing*. New York, NY: Avery Publishing Group Inc.

Belfield, Wendell O., and Zucker, Martin. 1993. *How to Have a Healthier Dog*. San Jose, CA: Orthomolecular Specialties.

Lieberman, Shari, and Bruning, Nancy. 1990. *The Real Vitamin and Mineral Book*. New York, NY: Avery Publishing Group Inc.

Pitcairn, Richard H., DVM, PhD. 1995. *Natural Health for Dogs and Cats*. Philadelphia, PA: Rodale Press.

Schoen, Allen M., and Wynn, Susan G. 1998. *Complementary and Alternative Veterinary Medicine.* St. Louis, MO.

Volhard, Wendy, and Brown, Kerry. 1995. *The Holistic Guide for a Healthy Dog.* Book House.

Part II: Feeding Your Dog the Easy Way

[1] DEMYSTIFYING MYTHS ABOUT PROTEIN

www.purina.ca/Dogs/puppies.asp?article=471.

[2] Ibid.

[3] Allison JB, Wannemacher RW, Migilarese JF: Diet and the Metabolism of 2-Aminoflorene, Journal of Nutrition 52:415-425, 1954.

www.drjwv.com/care.php?view=protein.php.

www.purina.com/images/articles/pdf/NutritionandRenalFunction.pdf.

www.canismajor.com/dog/iamssym1.html#KIdney.

[4] www.thenutritionreporter.com.

[5] www.acsma.org/csmtdbt5.htm.

[6] www.working-retriever.com/library/dietper.html.

[7] www.workingretriever.com/library/dietper.html.

[8] www.acsma.org/csmtdbt1.htm.

[9] www.canoe.ca.

[10] "Dietary Taurine Deficiency and Dilated Cardiomyopathy in Dogs." www.vetmed.ucdavis.edu. www.vetmed.ucdavis.edu/CCAH/Update06-2/6-2_Taurine.html).

[11] The Importance of Animal-Based Protein in Iams Dog Foods. www.iams.com: http://iams.com/en_US/jhtmls/nutrition/sw_NutritionQuestions_qanswer.jhtml?speciescode=D&brandcode=I&localeid=en_US&pagetypeid=PN&questionid=317).

[12] www.helpinganimals.com.

[13] *Nutritional Adequacy of Vegetarian Diets.* www.burns-pet-nutrition.co.uk.

[14] www.peteducation.com.

Part III: Remedial Diets Made Simple

[1] www.wabre.org.

[2] Waltham site.

[3] www.v-e-t-s.co.uk/heart_disease%20dog.htm.

[4] www.v-e-t-s.co.uk/heart_disease%20dog.htm.

[5] http://animalpetdoctor.homestead.com/Heart.html

[6] www.mesavet.com/library/heartmeds.htm,
www.vetheart.com/diseases.html.

[7] Dietary Management of Clinical Disorders in Dogs

http://web.archive.org/web/20010308065032/
www.jivaonline.com/html/dietary_management_of_clinical.html.

Bovee,Kenneth C. DVM, MMedSc. *The Mythology of Protein Restriction for Dogs with Reduced Renal Function,* Life Stage Nutrition Proceedings, 1998 Purina Nutrition Forum.

Dietary Management of Chronic Polyuric Renal Failure.

http://web.archive.org/web/20050403183424/http://www.speedyvet.com/speedyvet/library.asp?page=9.

[8] www.geocities.com/Heartland/Plains/1151/LiverDisease.html.

www.cah.com/library/liver.html.

[9] www.peteducation.com/article.cfm?cls=2&cat=1578&articleid=313.

[10] www.canine-epilepsy.com/healthydiet.html.

[11] www.vetcontact.com/en/art.php?a=1268&t.

[12] Dr. Pinkston, DVM.—More info? Book title? Website?

[13] www.integratedhealth.com/infoabstract/glucosab.html.

[14] http://homepage.mac.com/sholland/Papers/fishoil.html.

Index

A

Aging. *See* Senior dogs
ALA (alpha-linolenic acid), 30–31
Allergies, 52, 165, 171–72, 173
Aloe, 103–4, 179
American Association of Feed
  Control Officials (AAFCO), 8
Amino acids, 17–18, 22
Animal Protection Institute
  (API), 8
Antibiotics, 177, 178, 197,
  201–2
Antihypertensive diuretics, 126
Antioxidants, 179, 196, 206,
  212. *See also individual
  antioxidants*
Appetite, loss of, 115–19
Apple cider vinegar (ACV), 51
Arginine, 157
Arthritis and joint problems
  blood sugar levels and, 165
  diet and, 170, 173, 180,
    181–84
  supplements for, 52, 170,
    184–86
  treatment of, 181
Aspirin, natural form of, 185
Autoimmune disorders, 209, 210

B

Bacteria. *See also* Antibiotics;
Probiotics
  canine digestive process and,
    15
  carbohydrates and, 26–27
  friendly, 201–2
  raw diets and, 57
Berte's Daily Blend, 77, 90, 97
Berte's Digestion Blend, 206
Berte's Green Blend, 44, 71, 90,
  103, 206
Berte's Immune Blend, 71, 77,
  94, 109
Berte's Probiotic Powder, 109
Berte's Ultra Probiotic Powder,
  50, 90
Berte's Zymes, 88, 201, 205
Beta blockers, 126
Bioflavonoids, 46, 47, 184–85
Bladder problems
  diagnosis of, 187–88
  diet and, 191–95
  supplements for, 53, 196–97
  symptoms of, 187–88
  treatment of, 191
  types of, 188–90
Blood sugar levels, 165

Bones. *See* RMBs
Bromelain, 185, 201
Brown, Steve, 15

C

Calcium, 22, 34–36, 39, 69, 72, 79–80, 97
Calcium oxalate crystals, 189, 193–94
Cancer, 53, 132–40
Carbohydrates
bacteria and, 26–27
blood sugar levels and, 165
cancer and, 132–33
canine digestive process and, 15–16, 23–24
in commercial dog food, 15–16, 24–25
danger of, 25–26
as energy source, 28
kidney problems and, 145–46
lactation and, 27
liver problems and, 153–54
pregnancy and, 27
puppies and, 27
in vegetarian diets, 111
working dogs and, 107
Cardiomyopathy, 125, 126, 128
Carnitine, 18, 131, 157, 167
Cholesterol, 29
Chondroitin, 170, 185
Chromium, 36, 167
Cod liver oil, 30

Cooked diets. *See also* Homemade diets
cancer and, 135–38
guidelines for, 72–73
heart health and, 127, 130
ingredients for, 74–76
sample, 76–77
supplements for, 77
travel and, 101–2
Copper, 36
COQ10, 131, 149, 196
Cornsilk, 197
Cranberry juice, 196
Cruft, Charles, 4
Cystine crystals and stones, 190

D

Denosyl, 157
Diabetes, 165, 167, 168
Diarrhea, 53, 89, 198, 205
Diets. *See* Cooked diets; Dog food, commercial; Homemade diets; Raw diets; *individual health conditions*
Digestive enzymes, 49, 50, 201
Digestive process, canine, 13–15
Digitalis glycosides, 126
Diuretics, 126
DMG, 166–67
Dog food, commercial
adding fresh food to, 78–81
carbohydrates in, 15–16, 24–25

history of, 4–12
as industry, 3–12
labeling of, 8–9, 10–11
marketing and, 4–8, 9
"natural," 11
nutrition and, 8–9, 10
opposition to, 11–12
"premium," 9
travel and, 102–3
veterinarians and, 6–7, 8, 10, 11, 12
Dulce, 98

E

Ear infections, 54
Edema, 126
Enzymes, 185. *See also* Digestive enzymes
EPI (exocrine pancreatic insufficiency), 200
Epilepsy, 54, 165, 166–67, 168
Ewer, R. F., 13
Exercise, 118

F

Fats
cancer and, 133–34
deficiency of, 30
as energy source, 106
fatty acids, 30–31
guidelines for, 32
heart health and, 128–29
importance of, 29, 33
improper digestion of, 32
kidney problems and, 145
liver problems and, 154
pancreatitis and, 160
types of, 29–30
Fiber, 153–54
First aid, 103–4
Fish oil, 30, 71
Flexile Plus, 109
Folic acid, 97

G

Garlic, 51
Gastric problems
causes of, 198–99
diagnosis of, 199–200
diet and, 202–5
remedies for, 205
supplements for, 53, 205–6
symptoms of, 198
treatment of, 201–2
Glucosamine, 170, 185
Glutamine, 164, 185, 202

H

Halo Derma Dream, 104
Heart disease
diagnosis of, 123
diet and, 127–30
prevalence of, 123
stages of, 123–24
supplements for, 53, 130–31
treatment of, 125–26

types of, 124–25
Heart murmurs, 124–25
Herbs, immune-boosting, 212
HGE (hemorrhagic gastroenteritis), 200
High blood pressure, 126
Homemade diets
    benefits of, 57
    equipment for, 58–59
    guidelines for, 61–62
    ingredients for, 59–61
    switching to, 63, 81, 87–88
    travel and, 101–2
    variety in, 62–63
Hypertension, 126
Hypertrophic cardiomyopathy (HCM), 125, 126, 128
Hypothyroidism, 54, 165, 167–68

I

IBD (irritable bowel disease), 199
Immune system disorders
    autoimmune, 209, 210
    causes of, 208–9
    diagnosis of, 207
    diet and, 211
    overactive, 209
    supplements for, 211–12
    symptoms of, 207
    treatment of, 209–11
    types of, 208–9
    underactive, 208–9

Incontinence, 190
Iodine, 37
Iron, 37–38, 97

J

Joint problems. *See* Arthritis and joint problems

K

Kennel cough, 54
Kibble. *See* Dog food, commercial
Kidney problems
    diagnosis of, 142
    diet and, 144–48
    online resources for, 141, 149
    phosphorus and, 144, 145–46
    protein and, 20, 93–94, 145
    sodium and, 144
    supplements for, 53, 148–49
    symptoms of, 141
    types of, 142–43
Kidney stones. *See* Urinary tract crystals
Kronfeld, D. S., 20

L

Lactating dogs, 27, 95
L-arginine. *See* Arginine
Lavender oil, 104
L-carnitine. *See* Carnitine
L-glutamine. *See* Glutamine
Liver problems
    causes of, 151

diagnosis of, 150–51
diet and, 152–56
supplements for, 156–57
symptoms of, 150
treatment of, 151–52
Liver squares, 138
Low-glycemic diets
with low fat, 166–70
with regular fat, 170–75

M
Magnesium, 38
Manganese, 38, 170, 185
Meals, number of, 62, 63
Medications
difficulty with, 117
for heart disease, 126
liver problems and, 152
Milk thistle, 157
Minerals, 34–44, 69, 112–13.
See also individual minerals
Morris, Mark, 8
Motion sickness, 54

N
NAG (N-acetyl glucosamine),
202
National Research Council
(NRC), 8–9, 24

O
Oatmeal-based shampoos, 179
Omega-3 fatty acids, 30–31, 96,
131, 148

Omega-6 fatty acids, 30–31
Overfeeding, 62
Overweight dogs, 31–32, 93,
127–28

P
Pancreatitis
causes of, 159
diagnosis of, 158
diet and, 160–64
supplements for, 54, 164
symptoms of, 158
treatment of, 160
types of, 159–60
Papain, 185
Pet Food Institute, 7, 10
Phosphorus, 39, 69, 144,
145–46
Picky eaters, 67, 115–19
Pills. *See* Medications
Pitcairn, Richard, 67
Potassium, 40
Pregnancy, 27, 95–100
Probiotics, 49, 50, 177, 178, 197
Protein. *See also* Amino acids
cancer and, 133
composition of, 17–18
guidelines for, 22
heart health and, 128
importance of, 14, 17, 106,
128
kidney problems and, 20,
93–94, 145
liver problems and, 152–53

for puppies, 21, 89–90
quality of, 18–20
for senior dogs, 20–21, 92–94
sources of, 17, 21
soy, 112
vegetarian diets and, 111–12
Puppies. *See also* Pregnancy
   appetite loss in, 118–19
   carbohydrates for, 27
   guidelines for, 91
   protein for, 21, 89–90
   RMBs for, 86–87
   supplements for, 90
   transitioning, from
     commercial to homemade,
     87–88
   transitioning, to adult diet, 86
   with upset stomach, 88–89
   weaning, 83–86
Purina Company, 6
Purine crystals and stones, 190

R
Raw diets. *See also* Homemade
diets
   bacteria and, 67
   benefits of, 70
   cancer and, 134–35
   gastric problems and, 203–4
   guidelines for, 66–69
   heart health and, 127, 129
   ingredients for, 64–66
   sample, 69–70
   supplements for, 70–71

switching to, 66–67, 71, 117
temperature of food for, 67,
   117
travel and, 101–2
Rescue and Relief Essence, 98,
   104
Riboflavin, 113
RMBs (raw meaty bones), 35,
   65–66, 68, 86–87

S
Salmon oil. *See* Fish oil
SAM-e, 157
Sea vegetables, 41–44
Selenium, 40
Senior dogs
   feeding, 92–94
   with heart disease, 123, 125
   with kidney problems, 93–94
   protein for, 20–21, 93–94
   supplements for, 94
Shampoos, oatmeal-based, 179
Sheffy, Ben, 9
SIBO (small intestinal bacteria
   overgrowth), 200
Skin problems, 53, 175–79
Sodium, 127–28, 144
Soy products, 112
Spratt, James, 4–5
Steroids, 177
Stool-eating, 26–27
Stress, 115, 211
Struvite crystals, 189, 192–93
Supplements. *See also individual*

supplements and health conditions
  for cooked diets, 77
  definition of, 45
  for raw diets, 70–71

T
Tasha's Tummy Traveller
  Formula, 103
Taurine, 18, 131
Taylor, Beth, 15
Thayer's Witch Hazel with Aloe,
  103–4
Thyroid issues, 37
Travel, 101–4, 138–39

U
Urinary tract crystals, 187,
  188–90, 192–94
Urinary tract infections (UTIs),
  187, 188

V
Vaccinations, 208, 211
Vegetables
  cancer and, 132–33
  canine digestive process and,
    16
  ground, in small quantities,
    28, 68

  protein from, 19–20
  sea, 41–44
Vegetarian diets, 110–14
Vitamins
  A, 48, 49, 98, 113
  B complex, 46, 47, 113
  B_2 (riboflavin), 113
  B_9 (folic acid), 97
  C, 11, 46, 47, 98
  D, 36, 48, 49, 98, 113
  E, 11, 48, 49
Vomiting, 89, 198, 205

W
Water
  retention, 126
  for working dogs, 106–7
Whelp Help, 98
Willow bark, 104, 185
Witch hazel, 103–4, 179
Working dogs, 105–9

Y
Yeast, 165, 172, 173
Yucca, 170, 185

Z
Zinc, 41, 212

Acknowledgments

I would like to thank Brenda Jones for thinking up the K9Nutrition Yahoo group, which brought together a group of people to share thoughts and experiences on diets for dogs, and Mary Straus for her emphasis on research and attention to detail. Other sources of useful information include Gil Ash, Sharon Ogilvie, Mindy Fenton, Christie Keith, Shari Mann, Lisa Edwards, Amy Cavender Turpin, Tracey Rentcome, Shannon Watts, and the many people who participated regularly on K9Nutrition. This community showed real dedication to canine health and diet issues and a vital willingness to share their knowledge.

My family has been important in writing this book. I would like to thank my sister, Tennille Olson, for always encouraging me to write a book. I want to thank my husband, Jeff Shaver, for spending many hours reading the finished product. And lastly, I offer thanks to my late father, Clifford Olson, who was always there with his love, support, and confidence in my various projects over the years.

I want to thank Pete Nicholson for putting several of the articles I had written over the years in order and bringing this book together. Brenda Warner, Bridget Moran, Sharon Ogilvie, and Toni Skiles each helped shape the material into the book it is today.

Lastly, I would like to thank Bill Stranger. He saw the potential for this book, became my agent, and made the dream a reality.

About the Author

L ew Olson has shown and raised dogs since 1974. Olson graduated from the University of North Dakota in 1983 and moved to Austin, Texas, to attend graduate school at the University of Texas. In 1992 she switched all of her dogs over to a raw diet and observed considerable health benefits. In 1999, she started a Yahoo! Group called K9Nutrition. Lew has designed several nutritional supplement blends for dogs under the name of Berte's Naturals. She has written nutrition articles for several dog publications, including *The New Zealand Dog Gazette, The Rottweiler Quarterly, Mein Hund Naturich Gesund, The Total Rottweiler,* and numerous other magazines and newsletters. She is currently President of the Conroe Kennel Club and the Texican Rottweiler Club. She is an AKC judge, and exhibits her Rottweilers at AKC shows. Olson lives in Magnolia, Texas.